# DRAWING NEAR TO GOD

*Daily Meditations for Spiritual Refreshment*

GARY DELASHMUTT

Copyright © 2024 by Gary DeLashmutt
All rights reserved.
Printed in the United States of America
Published by New Paradigm Publishing
Columbus, Ohio

All rights reserved. No part of this publication may be reproduced, stored in a retrieval system, or transmitted in any form by any means, electronic, mechanical, photocopy, recording, or otherwise, without the prior permission of the publisher, except as provided for by USA copyright law.

Unless otherwise indicated, scripture quotations taken from the (NASB®) New American Standard Bible®, Copyright © 1960, 1971, 1977, 1995 by The Lockman Foundation. Used by permission. All rights reserved. lockman.org

Scripture References marked NIV are from NIV® Bible (The Holy Bible, New International Version®, NIV®). Copyright © 1973, 1978, 1984, 2011 by Biblica, Inc.™ Used by permission. All rights reserved worldwide.

Scripture references marked NLT are from *The Holy Bible, New Living Translation*, copyright © 1996, 2004. Used by permission of Tyndale House Publishers, Inc., Wheaton, IL, 60189. All rights reserved.

Trade paperback ISBN: 978-0-9976057-8-5

# ADVANCED PRAISE

Few things edify and enrich our souls as much as writing that comes from a careful study of scripture and that vibrantly applies scripture to the complex realities of contemporary life. This is what Gary DeLashmutt's book does. It can serve as an inspiring supplement, not a substitute, to our own reading of the scriptures. Highly recommended, especially for those who are committed to a life of service.

**Ajith Fernando**
Teaching Director of Youth for Christ in Sri Lanka, and author of *Joyful Perseverance: Staying Fresh through the Ups and Downs of Ministry*

*Drawing Near to God* is a powerful and transformative guide for anyone seeking a deeper relationship with the Lord. Each day's reflection and prayer are steeped in biblical wisdom, leading readers to a greater understanding of God's Word and His boundless love. The insights are both profound and practical, making this devotional an invaluable resource for spiritual growth. I wholeheartedly recommend it to all my friends and family, confident that it will bless and enrich their walk with God.

**V. Elizabeth Perkins**
Co-President, John & Vera Mae Perkins Foundation

Within these pages you will find authentic encouragement for both your heart and mind. The words and insights ring with authenticity because they resonate with God's revealed truth and also with real human experience. But there is even more beneath what you read on these pages. Behind the written words is an authentic man of God who humbly lives the words he writes. Gary is the real deal. In 2003, Gary generously welcomed me into his life and the life of his family and friends. Ever since, I have benefitted immensely from his wise insights, humble presence, and faithful friendship. Reading and meditating upon Gary's insights in this latest volume will help each of us delight in that which brings Gary delight—living together as faithful plodders in the Lord's very good work.

**Todd Stewart**
Co-Pastor of The Village Church, and Student Support Specialist at Manhattan High School

# CONTENTS

| | | |
|---|---|---|
| PROLOGUE | | 9 |
| 1. | YOUR SECRET RELATIONSHIP WITH GOD | 11 |
| 2. | SEE, FEEL, ACT | 15 |
| 3. | MOST PEOPLE'S LOVE WILL GROW COLD | 19 |
| 4. | SOME WERE DOUBTFUL | 23 |
| 5. | ONE THING IS NECESSARY | 27 |
| 6. | SHAMELESS AUDACITY | 31 |
| 7. | THE PRIVILEGES OF OUR JUSTIFICATION | 37 |
| 8. | EAGERLY WAITING FOR HEAVEN | 41 |
| 9. | THE GOD OF HOPE | 45 |
| 10. | SPIRITUAL SELF-DECEPTION | 49 |
| 11. | GRUMBLING AND DISPUTING | 53 |
| 12. | CITIZENS OF HEAVEN | 57 |
| 13. | ANXIOUS FOR NOTHING | 61 |
| 14. | THE PEACE OF CHRIST | 65 |
| 15. | BE FILLED WITH THE SPIRIT | 69 |
| 16. | FIGHT THE GOOD FIGHT | 73 |
| 17. | THE FEAR OF DEATH | 77 |
| 18. | RUNNING THE RACE | 81 |
| 19. | DIVINE DISCIPLINE | 85 |
| 20. | DON'T QUIT | 89 |
| 21. | THE PRAYER OF A RIGHTEOUS PERSON | 93 |
| 22. | LOVE COVERS OVER A MULTITUDE OF SINS | 97 |

| | |
|---|---|
| 23. WHY DOES GOD LOVE ME? | 101 |
| 24. READY FOR EVERY GOOD DEED | 105 |
| 25. MY WORD WILL NOT RETURN EMPTY | 109 |
| 26. DON'T CALL EVERYTHING A CONSPIRACY | 113 |
| 27. DISCOURAGEMENT | 117 |
| 28. PRIDE AND HUMILITY | 121 |
| 29. SERVING GOD IN OLD AGE | 125 |
| 30. HOW GREAT ARE YOUR WORKS | 129 |
| 31. IS THIS NOT A BURNING STICK? | 133 |
| ENDNOTES | 137 |

# PROLOGUE

When God speaks through His Word, it's like gold ore mined from a rock (Psalm 119:72, 127). I wrote these reflections because they have gladdened my heart and nourished my soul. I hope that they build you up as well.

My goal is more ambitious than this, however. I also hope this book motivates you to "mine more gold" yourself, because better than reading someone else's biblical reflections is reflecting on biblical passages through which God has spoken personally to you. Here are some things that have helped me over the years to be a more effective "miner" of God's word:

- I pray briefly before I read Scripture that God will open my eyes to behold wonderful things in His Word (Psalm 119:18). I use my mind when I study Scripture, engaging the text with disciplined curiosity. But I remember that the ultimate Teacher is the Holy Spirit, who illuminates His Word so that it "lights up" to me (1 Corinthians 2:12).
- As I read, I engage in "double listening." I try to listen carefully to what the passage is saying. Some basic inductive questions are helpful here. But while I do this, I am also

listening for a verse, or phrase, or even a word that arrests my attention (Luke 24:27, 32). Sometimes, writing out the passage slows me down and helps me to listen carefully.

- When a specific truth arrests me, I linger there. I re-read it carefully. I consider other passages that speak of the same truth. I ask God what this truth says to my current situation. I come back to this same passage later, and maybe memorize it so that I can carry it around with me through the day. Like a bee, I am trying to suck every bit of nectar from this flower. And as I do this, I thank God for illuminating His truth to me.

- Then I write down in a brief note what God has taught me, and how it has impacted me. This exercise helps me to process this truth more fully. I keep this note with other similar notes on other biblical passages. Later, I re-read these notes, and this often re-ignites these truths in my heart.

- Finally, I am attentive to how God might want me to use this truth to encourage someone in my life (Isaiah 50:4). When I share this truth to build someone else up, it also seems to go deeper into my own soul.

Reflecting on Scripture in this way has been one of the most rewarding exercises in my spiritual life. It gradually amasses a great treasure of inspired truth in my memory, which God's Spirit recalls at critical times. It trains my mind to think increasingly from God's perspective. And it stabilizes my heart with God's love and peace and joy. May God bless every effort that you make to reflect on His Word!

# 1

# YOUR SECRET RELATIONSHIP WITH GOD

**Matthew 6:6** "When you pray, go into your inner room, close your door and pray to your Father who is in secret—and your Father who sees what is done in secret will reward you."

Once we receive Jesus, we can build a deeply personal relationship with our Heavenly Father by talking with Him in private. Jesus calls this praying to God "in secret." Much in our relationship with the Father occurs privately between the two of us. Do you have this type of relationship with your Heavenly Father? Do you have special times connecting with Him that only you know about?

How wonderful to know that Jesus came to enable us to know *His* Father as *our* Father! When you put your faith in Jesus, God adopted you into His family (John 1:12), and He gave you His Spirit to enable you to relate to Him—as your loving Heavenly Father (Galatians 4:6).

Any healthy, close relationship has a private or "secret" aspect to it. This is what brings joy to such relationships: it is something special, just between the two of us. When this secret life withers, we know that intimacy is diminishing as well. In these situations, it becomes more important than ever to restore the relationship by spending time together—especially time alone.

It is the same with our relationship with our Heavenly Father. Just as an iceberg has most of its mass underwater, our secret relationship with God can and should be greater than our public spiritual lives. If we neglect this secret time, our spiritual lives will become like a sinkhole that gradually erodes underground until it eventually collapses in on itself—most often in moral failure. Our secret time with God helps us to avoid these kinds of devastating collapses. The healthy abundance of a secret life with God makes us much less vulnerable to the empty promises of sin.

God meets with us during these secret times, and He will "reward" us for our time together. Jesus clearly views this reward as highly desirable. He speaks of it as a clear encouragement to pray to our Father in secret. But what specifically is this reward? The immediate context suggests at least three different kinds of reward:

**1. We gain protection from the soul-destroying bondage of living for the approval of others.** Jesus says, "Beware of practicing your righteousness before people to be noticed by them" (Matthew 6:1). Our sinful nature thirsts for others to notice us— to gain their approval, admiration, and recognition. This deep compulsion emerges so naturally from our corrupted souls that very often we are unconscious of it.

Nothing counteracts our hunger for approval more effectively than times of secret fellowship with the Father. We can only solve superficial problems with superficial cures. But how do you cure the vacant hole in the human heart? Our insecurity runs so deep that nothing less than the infinite love of God can bring the security that we desperately need. With our need for approval met by the Father, we no longer need to perform for others or compare ourselves with them. Divine love strengthens us to genuinely serve others, rather than needing their recognition or avoiding their disapproval.

**2. We gain greater confidence that God cares deeply about us and wants to meet all of our needs.** God already knows our needs. But He wants us to develop a relationship of dependence, where we regularly ask Him to meet our physical, relational, and spiritual needs (Matthew 6:8, 11-13). Our secret time with God includes times of pouring our hearts out to Him, asking Him to meet the needs that we cannot. Every day brings a fresh batch of needs. Unless we unload these burdens onto God, they accumulate in our souls. They ignite anxiety, frustration, and self-sufficient strategies to meet them ourselves. But when we take our current needs to Him in private prayer, we experience fresh assurance that He cares for us as our loving Heavenly Father. During these times, we experience God's wise answers to our secret requests. This helps us to live securely as His dearly loved children, rather than like orphans who must protect and provide for themselves.

**3. We experience answers to kingdom-expansion prayers.** Jesus urges us to pray for the advancement of God's kingdom—that more people will come to know Him and more of His children will follow Him more closely (Matthew 6:9-10). As we spend secret time with our Father, His Spirit teaches us how to pray for the effective advancement of His kingdom. These answers become precious gifts in our secret relationship with Him. As you pray in secret, you will increasingly see God answer your prayers in the lives of others.

Sometimes, God asks us to keep these answers secret from other people, so that we don't misuse them as a way to boast. At other times, however, He urges us to share these answers as encouragement to our brothers and sisters in Christ. Over time, our confidence in the reality of intercessory prayer increases. This leads to a stronger desire to meet with our Heavenly Father for these special times of prayer alone with Him.

*Father, thank You that through Jesus You have made me Your child, and that I can now have a rich personal relationship with You. Teach me how to commune with You in secret. Make my secret times with You the richest parts of my day. Thank You for promising to reward my secret times with You—what amazing generosity!*

# 2

# SEE, FEEL, ACT

**Matthew 9:36-38** Seeing the people, Jesus felt compassion for them, because they were distressed and downcast like sheep without a shepherd. Then He said to His disciples, "The harvest is plentiful, but the workers are few. Therefore beseech the Lord of the harvest to send out workers into His harvest."

This passage captures the motivational dynamic that characterized Jesus' life and public ministry. Namely, what Jesus *saw* about the human condition apart from God affected what He *felt* concerning them, which motivated Him to *act* in certain ways.

Jesus *saw* that the people were "distressed and downcast like sheep without a shepherd." Without a shepherd to guide them, sheep face danger, difficulty, and confusion. Without God, humans confront a similar vulnerability: they are spiritually lost. In context (Matthew 8-9), Jesus encountered many people who were afflicted with various problems, including physical sickness and demonic possession. Jesus saw these conditions as symptoms of what happens to people when they live apart from God's loving leadership. But He also saw these same people as a "harvest." These were people who were willing to be gathered into God's kingdom.

What Jesus *saw* ignited what He *felt*. Jesus was not cold or detached or dispassionate. He felt intense compassion for the people's plight. The Greek word for "compassion" (*splagchnizomai*) literally means "to be moved as to one's bowels." When we experience intense emotions, it affects our physical bodies. This is why we speak of a deep disappointment as "heartbreaking." Jesus' observation of the human condition affected Him straight down into His body and soul.

What Jesus *saw* and *felt* motivated Him to *act* in certain intentional and constructive ways. What was His first action? Prayer. He urged His disciples to pray earnestly for God to send more workers to gather these people into His kingdom. In the very next chapter, He acted by sending His disciples to various villages to invite people to enter God's kingdom through faith in Him (Matthew 10).

*See-Feel-Act.* This pattern characterized Jesus throughout His public ministry.[1] When a rich man asked Jesus how to inherit eternal life, Mark recorded His reaction: "*Looking* at him, Jesus *felt* a love for him and *said* to him, 'One thing you lack: go and sell all you possess and give to the poor, and you will have treasure in heaven; and come, follow Me'" (Mark 10:21). Others may have seen a secure and confident man, but not Jesus. He saw a man filled with insecurity concerning life's most important issue—where he would spend eternity. What Jesus saw in this man moved Him to feel a deep love for him. And this motivated Jesus to speak certain words to this man. It's true that Jesus' words were painful. They exposed the man's trust in his riches. But they were ultimately an invitation to become truly rich by following Jesus.

What does this *See-Feel-Act* pattern mean for you and me? It means that we can be confident that this is how Jesus relates to each of us. He sees our true condition, even if we do not always see it. He sees that we are like sheep without a shepherd—lost and unable to make our lives work without His leadership. It means that Jesus feels real compassion for us—a deep concern for our plight and an intense desire to rescue and heal us. And it also means that Jesus has done something about our condition. He volunteered to carry the cross, to pay the penalty for our sins, and to issue eternal life to anyone who entrusts themselves to Him.

This *See-Feel-Act* pattern is also the way Jesus teaches us to live once we come to know Him and follow Him. When the apostle Paul was in Athens, he didn't just see a city full of culture, wealth, and highly educated people. He saw a "city full of idols" (Acts 17:16). He knew these false gods would never meet the deepest needs of the Athenians.

And what Paul *saw* affected how he *felt*. Paul's "spirit was being provoked within him." The Greek word for "provoked" (*parōxyneto*) is the Greek word from which we get the term "paroxysm," which is a powerful negative reaction. Paul allowed the pain of the Athenians to fill his heart. And what Paul *saw* and *felt* motivated him to *act* in a redemptive way. He went on to "reason with the Jews and the God-fearing Gentiles [about the reality of Jesus], and he spoke daily in the public square to all who happened to be there" (Acts 17:17 NLT).

What do you *see* when you look at the people around you? Are they people who really know how to have a good time? Are they an obstacle to your goals? Are they ideological enemies? Or are they people lost without hope and without God? (Ephesians 2:12)

What do you *feel*? Envy? Attraction? Fear? Annoyance? Vulnerability? Or do you feel compassion for how false gods are injuring them?

How do you *act*? By joining them? By politely dismissing them? By withdrawing from them? By self-righteously judging them? Or by showing and speaking God's love to them?

This is how Jesus saw you, felt about you, and acted toward you. And now, He lives within you to enable you to see and feel and act this same way toward others!

*Lord Jesus, thank You for seeing my true spiritual condition. Thank You for feeling compassion toward me. And thank You most of all that You died on the cross to rescue me. Open my eyes today to see others like sheep without a shepherd. Move my heart today to feel true compassion for them. Guide me today to communicate Your love to them through all that I do and say. Amen.*

# 3

# MOST PEOPLE'S LOVE WILL GROW COLD

**Matthew 24:12** "Because lawlessness is increased, most people's love will grow cold."

Jesus predicted that before history comes to a close the hearts of most human beings will become insensitive, calloused, and cold. Why would this happen? Jesus attributes this to "lawlessness."

The Greek word for "lawlessness" (*anomia*) literally means "no" (*a*) and "law" (*nomos*). It refers to a contempt, not just for civil law, but for God's moral imperatives. The idea is not simply that there will be lots of criminal activity at the end of the age. Most people will reject any notion of objective morality or truth.

The result? In the immediate context, Jesus speaks of His followers being persecuted (Matthew 24:9), and some will renounce their faith in Christ (Matthew 24:10). To make the situation worse, false prophets will mislead many people during this time (Matthew 24:5). This loss of both moral and spiritual truth will lead to anarchy. The apostle Paul describes this terrible situation in more detail. He writes, "In the last days dangerous times will come. People will be lovers of self, lovers of money, boastful, arrogant, revilers…

unloving, irreconcilable, malicious gossips, without self-control, brutal, haters of good, treacherous, reckless, conceited, lovers of pleasure rather than lovers of God" (2 Timothy 3:1-4).

When people contemptuously dismiss what God says is good, genuine love evaporates and human society becomes a hotbed of hostility and danger. With God out of the picture, who (or what) will fill the gap? It's no wonder that Paul says that people will love themselves, their money, and their various pleasures. As a result, they will become irreconcilable, brutal, treacherous, and reckless.

I do not know if we are living at the end of this age. For hundreds of years, many sincere followers of Jesus have concluded this. And they have been wrong. Maybe this is why Jesus warned us, "Of that day and hour no one knows, not even the angels of heaven, nor the Son, but the Father alone" (Matthew 24:36).

That being said, I do know that we are living in a culture that has largely rejected the concept of objective truth. For over half a century, postmodern philosophers and educators have ridiculed the notion of objective truth. Consequently, since there is no such thing as truth, human relationships ultimately distill down to the will to power—not love.

Moral anarchy has indeed increased to an unprecedented degree in our own society. As a result, most people's love has grown cold. Why should we be surprised at how brutal social media has become? Why should we be shocked that politicians justify self-promotion and blatantly slander others to advance their own agendas? Why should we think it strange that anxiety and depression are epidemic in our society? Love, commitment, and self-sacrifice collapse in a world where relativism replaces the moral foundation. As Jesus predicted, when lawlessness increases, the result is a cold, lonely, and dangerous world.

In a lawless and unloving society, God's people must do more than argue for the reality of objective truth and communicate that truth. We must also *demonstrate* what genuine love looks like. To rephrase Jesus' statement in Matthew 24:12, if we want people to turn away from lawlessness, we must fan the flames of our love.

Maybe this is why the authors of the New Testament letters, writing to Christians who lived in a lawless society, placed such a strong and repetitive emphasis on genuinely loving one another and on showing good will toward the non-Christians among whom they lived. Peter writes,

"Fervently love one another from the heart" (1 Peter 1:22).

"Keep your behavior excellent among [non-Christians], so that in the thing in which they slander you as evildoers, they may because of your good deeds, as they observe them, glorify God in the day of visitation" (1 Peter 2:12).

"Such is the will of God that by doing what is good you may silence the ignorance of foolish men" (1 Peter 2:15).

"Keep a good conscience so that in the thing in which you are slandered, those who revile your good behavior in Christ will be put to shame" (1 Peter 3:16).

"Above all, keep fervent in your love for one another, because love covers a multitude of sins" (1 Peter 4:8).

Peter tells us to always be ready to explain why we place our hope in Jesus (1 Peter 3:15). But let us live in such a way that makes them curious enough to ask!

---

*Lord Jesus, thank You that I do not need to be surprised about the lawlessness and lovelessness of our culture. Thank You also that I do not need to be cynical or despairing about this situation. Empower me to genuinely love my Christian brothers and sisters, so that people see that a community of love is possible. Empower me to show genuine goodwill toward those who do not believe in You, so that they may see that You have goodwill toward them. Give me courage to share with them the reason that I live this way—because You exist, You have loved me, and You have changed my life by Your love.*

# 4

# SOME WERE DOUBTFUL

**Matthew 28:16-20** The eleven disciples proceeded to Galilee, to the mountain which Jesus had designated. When they saw Him, they worshiped Him; but some were doubtful. And Jesus came up and spoke to them, saying, "All authority has been given to Me in heaven and on earth. Go therefore and make disciples of all the nations, baptizing them in the name of the Father and the Son and the Holy Spirit, teaching them to observe all that I commanded you; and lo, I am with you always, even to the end of the age."

Before Jesus ascended into heaven, He gave us the Great Commission. But have you ever noticed what Matthew says about the spiritual condition of some of Jesus' disciples when He gave this commission? Yes, they all worshiped the risen Jesus when He appeared to them in Galilee, but Matthew adds that "some were *doubtful*." Doubtful? Jesus was standing there in the flesh. What was there to be doubtful about? We can't know for sure, but exploring the likely answers may provide valuable encouragement to us.

It's hard to believe they doubted that Jesus physically rose from the dead. Of course, that was their immediate doubt when He appeared to them. Initially, the disciples thought Jesus was a ghost—so He invited them to touch His body, and He ate fish in their presence (Luke 24:36-43). Likewise, Thomas also doubted until Jesus appeared to Him and settled his doubts in a similar way (John 20:24-28). By the time Jesus appeared to them in Galilee, this doubt was most likely resolved. What then was the source of their doubt? Consider the following possibilities:

They may have doubted *the legitimacy of the mission*. This was not the only time that the resurrected Jesus gave them this commission. The gospel authors and the book of Acts record it (in various forms) five times. This amount of repetition not only emphasizes its importance; it also suggests the disciples' obtuseness. The disciples were slow to understand the primary step in Jesus' plan—namely, His death and resurrection. After all, they expected the Messiah to defeat His enemies, not be killed by them. Furthermore, they expected the nations to come to Israel, not for them to go to the nations. Right up to the day that Jesus ascended to heaven, they asked Him, "Is it at this time that You are restoring the kingdom to Israel?" (Acts 1:6) Many cultural and religious barriers could've raised doubts in their minds.

They almost certainly had doubts about *their adequacy for this mission*. After all, they had all forsaken Jesus when He was arrested. Peter's boast that He would never forsake Jesus had turned into emphatically denying Him (three times!) just a few hours later. Their egocentric hopes for positions of power in Jesus' kingdom had been crushed by His death (Mark 10:35-45). Now that Jesus had conquered death, why wasn't He telling them that *He* would go to every nation and call people to become His disciples? Why was He entrusting His world-wide plan to *them*?

They probably also had doubts about *the feasibility of this mission because of the implacable hostility of Jesus' enemies*. The Jewish leaders condemned Jesus as a false teacher, and they were still very much alive. Additionally, the Roman rulers hadn't gone anywhere, and they were the ones to execute Jesus. What would prevent them from executing the disciples? Without Jesus' physical presence, what chance would they have of extending His influence? They had no money, no military might, no political influence, and no social popularity. Some of His followers likely thought that the whole plan was doomed from the start.

Stop for a moment and consider how these same doubts often plague you and me today. Even though I can look back over the past 2,000 years and see that Jesus' commission has been substantially fulfilled, I often feel doubtful about my own role in His plan. Why would He choose me—especially with all of my past failures and present flaws? Is it really true that some people from every ethnic group will turn to Jesus as their Messiah? Some of them seem to be completely resistant. The rulers of this world are so powerful, and many of them are so evil. How can I bear witness to Christ amidst such strong opposition? Who am I to represent Jesus' values, especially when it undermines the values of the powerful?

This makes us greatly appreciate how Jesus responded to their doubts. He didn't *disqualify* them because of their doubts; instead, He included them *despite* their doubts. He was not repelled by their doubts; He drew near to them to minister to their doubts. This is just how Jesus responds to us when we meet with Him beset by doubts and fears concerning His mission. This is why Jesus bookended His commission with two great promises that were designed to strengthen our faith.

**Are you intimidated by the power and authority of our enemies?** Jesus said, "*All authority* has been given to *Me* in heaven and on earth." Jesus' authority will accompany us as we pursue His mission. He will either remove their opposition, or He will work through their opposition to advance His kingdom.

Think of Paul's imprisonments. In Philippi, Jesus sent an earthquake to release Paul *from* imprisonment, giving him an opportunity to witness to his jailer (Acts 16:25-30). But later in Rome, Jesus did not free him. Instead, He worked *through* Paul's imprisonment to spread His good news (Philippians 1:12). He used this as an opportunity for Paul to share the gospel to his Roman guards. He used Paul's writing ministry to send letters to convert and build up countless people down through the centuries.

**Are you afraid of being forsaken and overwhelmed by your own weaknesses?** Jesus responds, "I am with you always—even to the end of the age." Through His Spirit, Jesus is present with us in a way that is even greater than His physical presence during His public ministry (John 16:7). His Spirit will provide supernatural comfort when we suffer (2 Corinthians 1:3-5; 7:5-6); His Spirit will provide supernatural love to enable us to forgive our enemies (Acts 7:54-60); His Spirit will provide supernatural power to speak and act as God's representatives (Acts 1:8). As Corrie Ten Boom said about her ghastly time in a Nazi prison camp: "There is no hole so deep that God's love is not deeper still."

---

*Lord Jesus, thank You that You love me despite my doubts. Thank You that You chose me to represent You despite my doubts. Thank You for Your promises to lead me and be with me as I follow You with all of my flaws. Thank You for how You have proven Your faithfulness to me. Help me to remember Your promises as I follow You today.*

# 5

# ONE THING IS NECESSARY

> Luke 10:38-42 Now as they were traveling along, Jesus entered a village; and a woman named Martha welcomed Him into her home. She had a sister called Mary, who was seated at the Lord's feet, listening to His word. But Martha was distracted with all her preparations; and she came up to Him and said, "Lord, do You not care that my sister has left me to do all the serving alone? Then tell her to help me.'" But the Lord answered and said to her, "Martha, Martha, you are worried and bothered about so many things; but only one thing is necessary, for Mary has chosen the good part, which shall not be taken away from her."

Jesus defends and commends Mary for taking time out of her busy life to listen to His words. He also lovingly informs Martha that she would be in better shape if she followed Mary's example. This passage contains a valuable warning for us: *If we don't sit like Mary, we will serve like Martha.*

But don't be too hard on Martha. She is a good example in several ways. She invited Jesus into her home, and she practiced abundant hospitality by preparing a meal for Jesus and His disciples. In John

11, when Jesus visited after her brother Lazarus' death, Martha confessed her faith in Jesus as the Messiah. She also followed Him to Lazarus' tomb and witnessed Jesus as He brought Lazarus back from the dead. Martha was an active follower of Jesus, and we would do well to follow her example—with one exception.

Martha let her commendable service distract her from a far more important opportunity—to sit at Jesus' feet and listen to His words. The result was something that many active believers know by personal experience: She became "worried and bothered" (verse 41). Her service undoubtedly started out as an expression of love for Jesus. But it became tainted with anxious frustration. She became irritable toward her sister Mary for not helping her, and even toward Jesus for not telling Mary to help!

Our service for Jesus can become tainted by frustration, self-pity, and a critical spirit. During these times, we would do well to follow Jesus' three-fold instruction to Martha:

**1. "Only one thing is necessary."** What is the most important way you can influence others? According to Jesus, only one is essential: listening to Jesus' words. Yet, mere listening isn't enough. James writes, "Prove yourselves doers of the word, and not merely hearers who delude themselves" (James 1:22). We should do more than listen to Jesus, but certainly not less. After all, you can't be a doer of the word if you don't know it!

We serve Jesus in many good and faithful ways: reaching out to those who don't know Him yet, opening our homes to host others, being generous with our money, helping our brothers and sisters to mature in their faith—the list could go on. But the problem with the good is it can sometimes become the enemy of the great. When we allow service to edge out regular times of listening to Jesus' word, we shortchange ourselves. Our time with Christ is where we receive love and vitality and encouragement and guidance. All of this makes our service effective—for "apart from Me you can do nothing" (John 15:5). Because Mary sat at Jesus' feet, she was able to serve Him in a unique way at the proper time (see John 12:1-8).

2. **"Mary has chosen the good part."** The word "good" (*agathos*) has a superlative sense: this is the *best* part. Serving Jesus sometimes brings its own reward of experiencing God's power and seeing people change. But no service, no matter how exciting, is more satisfying than communing with Jesus by listening to His word. David said that God's words are "more desirable than much fine gold, and sweeter than honey" (Psalm 19:10). To learn about His great love for us, to receive insight into who we are, to learn about the kingdom He is preparing for us—these and many other things in God's word are the supreme privilege and delight of our lives in this present age.

3. **"Which will not be taken from her."** Listening to Jesus' words has a uniquely lasting impact. Most of what we currently value will go away: our beauty, our physical health, our possessions. These might slowly fade to dust throughout our lives, and they will certainly disappear at our death. However, our time spent with God can never be taken away from us. As Isaiah said, "The grass withers, the flower fades, but the word of our God stands forever" (Isaiah 40:8). Only God's word sticks with us throughout the day, throughout the years, and even throughout eternity. Only God's word ignites an eternal ripple effect in our lives by showing us the way to impact His eternal kingdom, and by shaping our souls into eternal Christlikeness.

---

*Lord, thank You that I can serve You by serving others. Thank You that when I become distracted by my service and frustrated with the people I serve, You gently remind me to come sit at Your feet and listen to Your word. Help me to prioritize this most precious of opportunities so my service for You and others is truly effective.*

# 6

# SHAMELESS AUDACITY

**Luke 11:5-13** Jesus said to them, "Suppose one of you has a friend, and goes to him at midnight and says to him, 'Friend, lend me three loaves; for a friend of mine has come to me from a journey, and I have nothing to set before him'; and from inside he answers and says, 'Do not bother me; the door has already been shut and my children and I are in bed; I cannot get up and give you anything.'"

"I tell you, even though he will not get up and give him anything because he is his friend, yet because of his persistence he will get up and give him as much as he needs. So I say to you, ask, and it will be given to you; seek, and you will find; knock, and it will be opened to you. For everyone who asks, receives; and he who seeks, finds; and to him who knocks, it will be opened.

"Now suppose one of you fathers is asked by his son for a fish; he will not give him a snake instead of a fish, will he? Or if he is asked for an egg, he will not give him a scorpion, will he? If you then, being evil, know how to give good gifts to your children, how much more will your heavenly Father give the Holy Spirit to those who ask Him?"

Jesus teaches us that three parties exist in every ministry situation. In this parable, there is the person in need of food (i.e. the guest), the person called upon to meet the need (i.e. the host), and finally, the one who can meet the needs (i.e. the neighbor). In the parable, God is the neighbor. He alone has the resources to meet the needs of others, and He chooses to do this through us. This parable, therefore, teaches us key aspects of meeting the needs of others in ministry. Jesus gives three essentials: (1) Be willing to serve, (2) acknowledge your helplessness, and (3) engage God with shameless audacity.

**1. Be willing to serve.** In the ancient world, very few inns existed, and travelers couldn't predict their schedules with any measure of reliability. This is one reason why hospitality was a solemn duty. Thus, in the ancient world, a "visitor was to be welcomed and cared for, regardless of the hour of his arrival."[2]

In the parable, the host could have put a pillow over his ears, ignoring the need at this late hour. But he acknowledged his responsibility to help. He pulled himself out of bed and opened the door to meet the need. This is the attitude of *willingness*.

On a daily basis, God sends people to you who have spiritual needs. Many we anticipate in our schedules, but many others are unexpected interruptions—much like the guest who came knocking at midnight. God wants to serve both types of people through us. Serving others is our greatest privilege and responsibility in life. Will you get out of bed when the need arises, or will you put a pillow over your ears? There are lots of ways to put a pillow over our ears.

- We can serve when it's convenient, but fundamentally reject serving others as a lifestyle responsibility.
- We can decide that we will not serve today—that today is a "me" day.
- We can decide to serve only those we expect, but not those who "interrupt" us.
- We can decide to serve only those who are in our close

circle of friends, but not those who are different from us.
- We can decide to serve only those whom we feel competent to serve, not those who are "over my head."

So, before we pray for help to love and serve others, we must begin with a willingness to serve. But it doesn't end there.

**2. Acknowledge your helplessness.** When the visitor knocks on the door late at night, the host says, "I have *nothing* to set before him." Not only does he lack bread; he doesn't even have flour! He goes to his neighbor because he knows very well that he is *absolutely helpless* to meet these needs. And he *expresses this helplessness* to his friend.

Honestly, this is your position in *every* situation when you're serving others. Are you sharing your faith with someone at the office? Spending quality time with your children or spouse? Preparing to teach others God's word? Visiting an ailing friend or loved one? All of these service opportunities have one thing in common: You have *nothing* to set before them. This is what Jesus means when He said, "Apart from Me, you can do nothing" (Jn. 15:5). We do not have the love or the wisdom or the power or the patience or the courage or the clarity of speech within ourselves. Only God has the spiritual life that others need. Our role? Acknowledge our utter helplessness *to ourselves* and *express this helplessness to Him*. Sometimes we can acknowledge this aloud, but more often, we express this silently to the Lord who hears us.

Some of us rarely pray in such situations. This must be because we don't believe we are helpless. Jack Miller describes his struggle in this area when he writes, "Increasingly I saw myself as a desperately needy person, like the man who goes to his friend at midnight and says, 'I have nothing.' Before this, my problem in praying was that I had something—namely, reliance on myself, my training, my study, and my work. But the man at midnight has *no* bread for himself or for others."[3]

Some of us know we have nothing, but we let our inadequacy paralyze us from going to God. Hallesby states:

> Do not become (discouraged) because of your helplessness. Above all, don't let it prevent you from praying. Helplessness is the real secret and impelling power of prayer... For it is only when we are helpless that we open our hearts to Jesus and let Him help us... according to His grace and mercy.[4]

So let us turn to God in every serving situation, both affirming our willingness to serve and admitting our helplessness. To these, add one final step.

**(3) Engage God with shameless audacity.** Why did the neighbor agree to get up and give the man as much as he needed for his guest? Stated simply, this man wouldn't take "No" for an answer. Jesus says that it was "because of his persistence" (verse 8). However, the translation "persistence" (*anaideia*) doesn't capture this unique Greek word. This word falls short in its translation. The NIV is closer with rendering this word as "shameless audacity." This is a bold term. It means "shamelessness," "impudence," or "without regard for etiquette." Jesus says we should pray like this in every ministry situation—with this same shameless audacity before God—expecting to receive what we ask for. Jesus said, "So... ask, and it *will* be given to you" (verses 9-10).

On what basis can we ask in this way? Does God answer such prayers because you have been such a perfect model of spiritual maturity recently? Is it because you hold some sort of specific leadership role? Is it because you have been particularly spiritually minded this week? Not according to this passage. We can turn to God with "shameless audacity" because God is our Father: "Suppose one of you fathers is asked by his son for a fish; he will not give him a snake instead of a fish, will he? Or if he is asked for an egg, he will not give him a scorpion, will he?" (verses 11-12)

Unlike the neighbor in the parable, God is *not* a reluctant helper. It is this *contrast* between the reluctant neighbor and God as our Father that Jesus emphasizes. God is our Father who is abundantly gracious and generous. He has promised to give His children everything we need to serve others, and He is delighted when we make bold prayers on the basis of our Father-child relationship with Him.

And what will our Father give us when we ask with willingness to serve and helplessness and shameless audacity? Jesus asks, "If you then, being evil, know how to give good gifts to your children, how much more will your heavenly Father give the Holy Spirit to those who ask Him?" (verse 13) Literally, the Greek reads: "How much more will He give Holy Spirit to those who ask Him." This lack of the definite article emphasizes the Spirit's *provision* rather than His Person. That is, He will give whatever provision is needed to enable us to serve. It may be courage, wisdom, discernment, patience, compassion, forgiveness, mercy, spiritual authority, or any other needed quality.

We don't even have to know exactly what we need. We just need to ask, and He will give us what He knows we need. This was the key to how Jesus served God so effectively—He asked for a fresh enablement from the Holy Spirit. And this is the key to effective service in our own lives!

We shouldn't wait until we *feel* He has answered such prayers. Rather, when we pray in this way, we can plunge into the situation and count on the divine fact that the Holy Spirit *will* give what He has promised. As Andrew Murray writes:

> As we pray to be filled with the Spirit, let us not seek for the answer in our feelings… [Rather] let [us] believe, the Father gives the Holy Spirit's [help] to His praying child… [In this way] the blessing, *which has already been given us*, and which we hold in faith, may break through and fill our whole being.[5]

*Heavenly Father, thank You for wanting to work powerfully through me as a loving agent in this world. Thanks that You care about these people in my life far more than me, sending Jesus to die on the Cross for each of them. Help me to view each day as a series of opportunities to see You answer big prayers to serve others. Thank You for giving me a life filled with the Holy Spirit's power. Amen.*

# 7

# THE PRIVILEGES OF OUR JUSTIFICATION

**Romans 5:1-5** Therefore, having been justified by faith, we have peace with God through our Lord Jesus Christ, through whom also we have obtained our introduction by faith into this grace in which we stand; and we exult in hope of the glory of God. And not only this, but we also exult in our tribulations, knowing that tribulation brings about perseverance; and perseverance, proven character; and proven character, hope; and hope does not disappoint, because the love of God has been poured out within our hearts through the Holy Spirit who was given to us.

What a gift to be justified by God! Through the work of the Cross, God legally and judicially acquitted us of all our guilt. Though we still fail on a daily basis, we have been declared, "Not guilty," by the only Judge whose verdict ultimately matters. Through Jesus, God gave us a permanent legal standing before Him.

If this was the only gift that God ever gave us, it would be utterly amazing.

But our justification is only the beginning. Our new legal standing with God serves as a key that opens a vault filled with many other divine gifts. Having resolved the problem of our moral guilt through Jesus' atoning death, God freely lavishes His riches upon us. Consider the gifts that flow from our justification:

**"We have peace with God."** Before we met Christ, we expressed ongoing hostility toward God because of our sins. He justly condemned us because we continued in our revolt against Him. But now, having been justified by God, a permanent peace treaty now prevails. We never need to worry that this treaty will be nullified. Our justification gives us an objective peace with God. This serves as the basis for enjoying the personal peace of God in our hearts (Philippians 4:7).

**"We have obtained our introduction."** You can't just walk into the presence of a king; you must first receive an "introduction." Because of our justification, we possess a personal access to God. Because we now stand in a reconciled relationship with God, He grants us the right to draw near to Him, to relate with Him, and to seek His help. This access isn't based on how righteously we have been living, or on how close to God we have been feeling. It is based solely on our justified status. It is based only on Jesus' finished work on our behalf. This access to God is not only for certain days or in certain settings. It is 24/7 access. You can come to God in any and every circumstance—in any and every condition.

**"We exult in the hope of the glory of God."** God's holiness is so glorious, and our sin is so odious that "no one can see God's face and live" (Ex. 33:20). Beholding the full glory of God would be our everlasting undoing. But because Jesus has justified us, we can now look forward confidently to the day when we will behold God's unshielded glory. Now, instead of that moment being the occasion for our eternal death sentence, it will be the completion of our salvation by God. We will possess glorious bodies like Jesus. In that great day, "we will be like Him, because we will see Him just as He is" (1 John 3:2). Jesus will "transform the body of our humble state into conformity with the body of His glory"

(Philippians 3:21).

**"We exult in our tribulations."** Now that we have been justified and God is our Friend and Ally, His sovereign wisdom and power work in every area of our lives—even using our suffering for good. We still suffer, and this will still hurt. But instead of only causing pain and sorrow, our sufferings now become means through which God develops in us precious qualities—new traits that we would not otherwise possess. God creates "perseverance" in our lives—the ability to endure and stay faithful through future difficulties. He produces "proven character" within us—the growth of our love for God and others and the purging of our inordinate desires. And finally, God grows "hope" within us—the unrelenting optimism that comes from knowing that God will have the final word.

**"The Holy Spirit has been given to us."** God has always wanted to indwell our souls so that we can experience His love—but our unresolved guilt made us objects of His righteous condemnation. But at the very moment of our justification, God's Spirit indwelled us and brought infinite reservoirs of His love. The Holy Spirit personally assures us of the reality of God's love. He makes the objective love of God a subjective experience (Romans 8:15-16). Out of this abundance, we can draw love for others—even our enemies. Now that we have this down-payment of God's love, we need not fear. We can be confident that one day we'll see God face-to-face and experience the fullness of His love.

*Thank You, Lord Jesus, that Your death for me has the power to justify me forever. Thank You that this justification is a free gift, received by simply holding up my empty hands of faith. Thank You that this justification opens the door to reconciliation, to bold access to You, to hope for the future, to ultimate good through all of my current suffering, and to the assurance of Your love through Your Spirit. I have an abundance of life far beyond what I could ask or imagine. Open the eyes of my heart to realize how wealthy I am. Help me to live today in light of this great wealth.*

# 8

# EAGERLY WAITING FOR HEAVEN

**Romans 8:18-25** I consider that the sufferings of this present time are not worthy to be compared with the glory that is to be revealed to us. For the anxious longing of the creation waits eagerly for the revealing of the sons of God. For the creation was subjected to futility, not willingly, but because of Him who subjected it, in hope that the creation itself also will be set free from its slavery to corruption into the freedom of the glory of the children of God. For we know that the whole creation groans and suffers the pains of childbirth together until now. And not only this, but also we ourselves, having the first fruits of the Spirit, even we ourselves groan within ourselves, waiting eagerly for our adoption as sons, the redemption of our body. For in hope we have been saved, but hope that is seen is not hope; for who hopes for what he already sees? But if we hope for what we do not see, with perseverance we wait eagerly for it.

The apostle Paul knew how to suffer. His persecutors tortured him, insulted him, and openly slandered him. In order to share the gospel, he needed to risk the danger of traveling in the ancient world, facing shipwreck on the open sea on multiple occasions. He carried around a "thorn in the flesh," which was probably some kind of chronic and very painful physical malady. Beyond all of this, he suffered the agony of experiencing others falling away from Christ or rejecting him altogether.

Yet Paul writes that his sufferings "are not worthy to be compared with" the magnificent beauty that will be revealed to him when Jesus returns.

What did Paul know about the next age that made his present sufferings seem minor by comparison? (v.18) What filled him with eager anticipation? (vv.24-25) For most Christians, the next life is vague and abstract—mostly or completely unlike this life. Such a vague abstraction possesses little power to ignite in us any sort of victorious hope. Paul viewed his suffering through the lens of a core and central truth: *Those who belong to Jesus will experience eternity in a renewed and restored physical world.*

The destiny of God's creation has always been bound to the human condition. The world would flourish under human stewardship as long as humans flourished under God's loving rulership (Genesis 1:28). But ever since the first humans rebelled against God, His creation has suffered because it cannot now be what it was designed to be (Genesis 3).

Since humans are now fallen and broken by our rebellion against God, creation is also broken, groaning under the weight of human sin. The physical world is "subjected to futility" (v.20) and "enslaved to corruption" (v.21). It metaphorically groans like a mother in childbirth, longing for the day when God's children will be the rulers they were designed to be (vv.22-23). When Jesus returns, He will give those who belong to Him new, resurrected physical bodies (Philippians 3:20-21). When this happens, the rest of creation will become all of what it was intended to be—beautiful, magnificent, bountiful, and enjoyable beyond our wildest imagination.

For Christians, this hope is not wishful thinking. Jesus' bodily resurrection serves as the preview and guarantee of what will happen to our bodies when He returns (1 Corinthians 15:20-23). And when we notice the Holy Spirit's transformation of our characters, we gain a very personal and subjective guarantee of what He will one day do with our bodies and with the whole created order (v.23).

Our heavenly hope is not abstract, but very common to our everyday experience. All of us understand what it is like to enjoy God's current creation with physical bodies. We experience this every day. We enjoy a tasty meal, a loving hug, a beautiful sunset, the scent of spring flowers or fall leaves, the sound of birds singing, the warmth of the sun, the caress of a cool breeze. Our hearts fill with awe and wonder when we see a mountain range or the ocean or the night sky.

What if we will not only enjoy perfect health, but also have an even greater ability to sense and enjoy God's creation? What if God's creation will one day not only be cleansed of all human pollution and exploitation, but will be even more gloriously beautiful than it is now? What if everything that we love about God's current creation will be accessible to us then—only filled with more awe and endless joy? Then, as C. S. Lewis says:

> The new earth and sky, the same yet not the same as these, will rise in us as we have risen in Christ. And once again… the birds will sing and the waters flow, and lights and shadows move across the hills, and the faces of our friends laugh upon us with amazed recognition.[6]

This is your future. This means that you can agree with Paul, when he writes, "For this hope we have been saved… (and) with perseverance we wait eagerly for it" (vv.24-25).

*Thank You, Lord Jesus, for being my great Savior and Healer. Thank You for coming to die on the cross to forgive the guilt of my sins. Thank You for sending Your Spirit to transform my heart and heal so much of my brokenness. Thank You that You will return to give me a new body with which to enjoy Your new heavens and earth. Open my mind and heart to the reality of this glorious future which You have promised me. Ignite within me the hope that overshadows my present sufferings, that I may serve You faithfully and joyfully until that day.*

# 9

# THE GOD OF HOPE

**Romans 15:13 NIV** May the God of hope fill you with all joy and peace as you trust in Him, so that you may overflow with hope by the power of the Holy Spirit.

What does God desire for His children? That we "overflow with hope." Since God is "the God of hope," we can experience a super-abundance of confidence concerning our future—despite the fact that we live in a profoundly broken world that many find hopeless. Indeed, even today, we can experience this overflowing hope within us to such an extent that some people will *ask* us about its source (1 Peter 3:15).

Paul had hope on his mind in Romans 15. He speaks about the Old Testament scriptures, which were given to us so that "we might have hope" (v.4). The Old Testament brings us hope because it predicts the coming of the Messiah—the One in Whom both Jews and Gentiles will place their "hope" (v.12). It is in the hope of Jesus that God wants our hearts to overflow. Because Jesus has already taken our sins on Himself on the cross, we can be confident that He will also return as our King to make all things new and right.

In the meantime, this hope can overflow in us because God can "fill us with all joy and peace." The more God's joy and peace fill our hearts, the more we can face the future with hope. Like spending time with close friends during a time of discouragement, God's joy doesn't *eliminate* sadness and anxiety, but it certainly *outweighs* it.

Jesus was the One to inaugurate this promise of a new and living hope. He promised that He was able to give His disciples a peace that outweighs the anxieties generated by this broken and hostile world. He said, "Peace I leave with you; My peace I give to you; not as the world gives do I give to you. Do not let your heart be troubled, nor let it be fearful… These things I have spoken to you, so that in Me you may have peace. In the world you have tribulation, but take courage; I have overcome the world" (John 14:27; 16:33). He also told His disciples that His words could give them a fullness of joy: "These things I have spoken to you so that My joy may be in you, and that your joy may be made full" (John 15:11).

No combination of self-help techniques can give what God desires for us. God gives us His peace, hope, and joy through "the power of the Holy Spirit." We cannot self-generate these blessings. But because the Spirit of God now lives within us, He is able to supernaturally ignite peace, hope, and joy in our souls. He is willing and able to bear these fruits within us, along with love, patience, kindness, gentleness, faithfulness, and self-control (Galatians 5:22-23). He is committed to growing these qualities so that they increasingly characterize our lives, so that He may demonstrate to the watching world how real and good Jesus is.

But what if you lack the peace, joy, and hope of God in your life? What if these are not an experiential reality for you? What then?

God's answer to you is that these blessings will appear "as you trust in Him." Trust in God cannot be reduced to an impersonal formula or an app! We are personal and relational beings, and we are called to relate to God on that level. And God is committed to teaching us how to trust in Him. How? The Bible suggests a number of ways that we grow in our ability to trust in God. Here are just a few of them:

**Spend time alone with God in prayer.** Pour out your current concerns to Him. Listen to whatever He may say to you. Express your praise and thanks as you reflect on all He has given to you. These frequent times of prayer boost our confidence that God is indeed our Father, our Refuge, and our Shepherd. This creates an environment of confidence in which peace, joy, and hope grow.

**Ponder and treasure God's words.** As God draws your attention to specific biblical passages, learn to rely increasingly on the truthfulness of His words—even when they contradict your own thoughts and feelings. God promises that trusting Him in this way will lead to genuine happiness in Him and stability (Psalm 1:1-3).

**Give His love away to the people He puts in your life.** A self-protective posture may seem reasonable in our cold-hearted world. But this ultimately increases our sadness, anxiety, and cynicism. Jesus invites you to follow a different way. Remember God's promises to care for you, and in light of these promises, be a servant to those around you. The more you do this, the more you will experience true happiness (John 13:1-3, 17).

---

*Lord Jesus, thank You that You desire to fill me with Your joy and peace, so that I may overflow with Your hope. Thank You for giving me Your Spirit, who lives in me to impart Your peace, joy, and hope. Thank You that, despite the waywardness of my heart, You love to teach me how to trust in You. Help me to see today how You are doing this.*

# 10

# SPIRITUAL SELF-DECEPTION

**1 Corinthians 3:18; 4:14** Do not deceive yourselves. If any of you think you are wise by the standards of this age, you should become "fools" so that you may become wise… I am writing this not to shame you but to warn you as my dear children.

Are you deceived about an issue in your life? If you were, how would you know? Since deception often comes from within, you cannot look within yourself for the solution. By definition, self-deception comes from a deceived self. So again, how do you know if you are deceived in a given area of your life?

One of the most sobering themes in the Bible is that fallen human beings are extremely vulnerable to spiritual self-deception. "Do not deceive yourselves," Paul said to the Corinthian Christians. Many of them had embraced a philosophy of life that was profoundly contrary to God's perspective. Yet they believed that they had become wise—even wiser than the apostle Paul, who had introduced them to Jesus and wrote half of the books in the New Testament! If you wonder how they could have gotten so far off course, you don't know yourself very well.

It would be nice if spiritual deception only came through one mode or means. But it doesn't. Spiritual deception enters our lives in a variety of ways. As you read through these passages, ask yourself: Is it possible that I'm self-deceived in any of these areas?

> Trust in the Lord with all your heart, and *do not lean on your own understanding.* ⁶ In all your ways acknowledge Him, and He will make your paths straight. ⁷*Do not be wise in your own eyes*; fear the Lord and turn away from evil (Proverbs 3:5-7).

Here Solomon warns his son against the deadly danger of assuming that he knows within himself the way to live his life.

> "The eye is the lamp of the body; so then if your eye is clear, your whole body will be full of light. ²³ But if your eye is bad, your whole body will be full of darkness. *If then the 'light' that is in you is darkness, how great is the darkness"* (Matthew 6:22-23).

In context, Jesus warns that pursuing materialistic values will distort our spiritual vision. But here's the worst part: At the very same time that our spiritual sensitivity is dulled, we will think that we see better than others. It is one thing to be blind and know it, but it is far more tragic to be blind and think that you see just fine!

> Jesus told this parable to some people *who trusted in themselves that they were righteous*, and viewed others with contempt (Luke 18:9).

Jesus reserves His harshest words for outwardly religious people. He does not do this because He hates them, but because He loves them. He knows that their self-righteousness has deceived them into thinking that they have merited God's acceptance. It may take painful exposure by Jesus to jolt us out of our self-righteous blindness into the sane awareness that we need to ask God for His mercy through Jesus.

> "I know your deeds, that *you have a name that you are alive, but you are dead.* ² *Wake up,* and strengthen the things that

remain… For I have not found your deeds completed in the sight of My God" (Revelation 3:1-2).

It's not unusual to find Christians resting on their laurels. Quite often believers in Jesus assume that they are currently spiritually healthy because their past service guarantees their spiritual health. What does Jesus say to such Christians? Wake up! What a timely word for those of us who are several decades into our Christian lives!

One of God's main means of protecting or rescuing us from spiritual self-deception is other Christians who love us enough to say something—to admonish and correct us in love (Ephesians 4:15). This is what Paul did for the Corinthian Christians. "I am writing this *not* to shame you, but to admonish you as my beloved children" (1 Corinthians 4:14). Paul did this by asking penetrating questions (1 Corinthians 4:7), and even resorting to godly sarcasm (see 1 Corinthians 4:8). Although they may have felt stung by his words, his intent was to wake them up so they could begin to prosper spiritually.

What good parent ever desires to bring pain to his children? But all good parents know that their children are sometimes foolish and veer into danger—all the while pridefully thinking they are safe. How blessed such children are to have parents who will take wise, timely, and (if necessary) painful measures to help them back on track.

God has put other Christians into our lives for this purpose. They can see what we do not currently see. They can sense the spiritual danger of which we are oblivious. They have words of truth that can wake us up—if only we are willing to listen to them! My own spiritual life has been rescued by such friends on many occasions. Maybe you can say the same thing. Or maybe you are in dire need of such a friend right now because you are drifting into spiritual danger without even knowing it.

A traffic light has three colored lights—green ("Go"), yellow

("Caution"), and red ("Stop"). What light are you flashing to your Christian friends? What posture do you present to your Christian friends?

- "Don't you dare reprove me. Mind your own business!" This is the norm for our culture. But according to Solomon, it is the posture of a fool (Proverbs 12:15).
- "You had better proceed with extreme caution!" We can wrongly demand that others correct us perfectly before we are willing to listen. But do we ever hold that same standard when they offer encouragement?
- "I trust that you love me, and I know that I can be deceived. So, please speak truth to me even if it hurts." This is the posture of wisdom—and it will lead to spiritual safety and even greater wisdom!

---

*Lord Jesus, thank You that You love me enough to admonish me. I would still be alienated from You if You had not shown me that I needed Your forgiveness. I would have made a terrible mess of my life if You had not corrected me many times. I know that I am vulnerable to spiritual self-deception. Help me to listen to the loving correction that You speak to me—either through Your Word or through Your children.*

# 11

# GRUMBLING AND DISPUTING

**Philippians 2:14-16** Do all things without grumbling or disputing; so that you will prove yourselves to be blameless and innocent, children of God above reproach in the midst of a crooked and perverse generation, among whom you appear as lights in the world, holding forth the word of life, so that in the day of Christ I will have reason to glory because I did not run in vain nor toil in vain.

Humanity lives in darkness. Apart from Jesus, human individuals and societies are "crooked and perverse." If God isn't in the center of our lives, then who or what will fill His place? Without Jesus, human egos bend inward—being fundamentally broken. Cut off from our Creator by our sins, we are self-centered rather than God-centered. As a result, we reap in our own lives and societies the damage of this way of life. Since this darkness is all that we've ever known, we are usually only dimly aware of what it is doing to us and others until we come to Jesus, the Light of the world.

Once we come to the Light of the world, He commissions us to be His lights in the world. Despite our continuing brokenness, He has decided to work through us to draw others to Himself. Even through our imperfect lives, He can display an attractive picture of how He designed humans to live. Through our lives, He can speak a compelling message that invites people in the dark to come to the warmth of His light.

**"Do all things without grumbling."** What an accurate description of the natural disposition of fallen human hearts! "Grumbling" is the inevitable outcome of people who focus on what they don't have. Grumbling comes naturally to people who don't know God or His love. Their happiness isn't tied to anything transcendent. So, their circumstances are all that they have to bring them happiness.

That's why grumbling about the boss is a perennially popular activity. That's why grumbling about our spouses and neighbors seems so justified. That's why people tend to grumble more as they get older. C. S. Lewis warned that unless we meet Jesus and follow Him, our lives will eventually become an interminable grumble!

The opposite of grumbling, of course, is gratitude. When lost people interact with God's people, one thing they should be struck by is how grateful they are. How intriguing and attractive it is to interact with people who have the same problems and challenges as everyone else, but who genuinely express gratitude. And it's no wonder. We have a personal relationship with the God who loves us, watches over us, and promises to do good to us.

But people are rarely interested in God unless our gratitude significantly outweighs their grumbling. Maybe this is why Paul devotes much of Philippians 4 to reminding us to rejoice in the Lord, to take our anxieties to Him with thankfulness, and to set our minds on all the good things He has given us. Grateful Christians expose the darkness by offering a positive contrast to the emptiness of life without God.

**"Do all things without… disputing."** Christians should dispute falsehood and seriously destructive behavior. But first and foremost, we are to be known as people who are easy to get along with, who contribute positively to our communities, and who are respectful and cooperative toward our work and civil authorities. No wonder Paul said later in this letter, "Let your forbearing spirit be known to all people" (Philippians 4:5). There is the great secret. The same Lord Jesus who has been so forbearing to me enables me to show His forbearance to others—no matter how annoying they may be.

Unfortunately, Christians in our culture have a reputation for being mean-spirited, argumentative, uncaring—even toxic. Although this reputation is not necessarily fair, it is true enough of the time to give Jesus a bad reputation. No wonder Paul says, "Don't add to the darkness with your own disputing. Let Jesus' patient love for all humanity shine through you!"

**"Holding forth the word of life."** Most English translations say, "holding fast the word of life." The word "holding forth" (*epechō*) can also be translated as "holding fast." The first translation would imply giving others the gospel, while the second implies holding it to ourselves.

The context suggests that "holding forth" is the more accurate translation. After all, Paul describes Christians as lights in the world who influence others toward Jesus. We are to *display* a grateful and cooperative spirit for this purpose. And we are to *hold forth* (or hold out) a message that invites people to meet Jesus. This is the message that says: "God loves you so much that He sent His Son to die for all of your sins. You can be reconciled with God, just as you are, by simply entrusting yourself to Jesus." Hold forth this message—wisely, patiently, and boldly—as the good news that it is. Let people know that whatever good they see in your life is because of Jesus' influence. And invite people to come to the living Jesus as the Light who will change their lives!

*Lord Jesus, thank You for bringing Your people across my path. Thank You for drawing my attention to their grateful and cooperative hearts. And thank You for empowering them to hold forth Your word of life to me. I am humbled that You want to shine Your light on others through me. I am aware of my many inadequacies—but I present myself to You today to "shine as a light."*

# 12

## CITIZENS OF HEAVEN

**Philippians 3:20-4:1 NLT** But we are citizens of heaven, where the Lord Jesus Christ lives. And we are eagerly waiting for Him to return as our Savior. He will take our weak mortal bodies and change them into glorious bodies like His own, using the same power with which He will bring everything under His control. Therefore, my dear brothers and sisters, stay true to the Lord.

The Romans had many colonies across their vast empire—one of which was Philippi. This provided many of the Philippians with the privilege of Roman citizenship. This afforded them significant legal rights and economic opportunities that non-citizens lacked. Most likely, several of the Philippian Christians possessed Roman citizenship, and many others wished they did.

Paul did not denigrate Roman citizenship. After all, he was himself a Roman citizen. On more than one occasion, he used this status to secure legal protection and due process (Acts 16:35-39; 25:10-12). Yet Paul makes it clear that even Roman citizenship is not an ultimate status for the follower of Jesus.

Christians belong to God's kingdom, and so our ultimate loyalty belongs to a different King—the Lord Jesus Christ. Furthermore, an inordinate love of our earthly citizenship is a spiritual trap that

Christians should avoid. This is why Paul begins verse 20 with the word "But." This contrasts what Paul wrote earlier:

> "I have told you often before, and I say it again with tears in my eyes, that there are many whose conduct shows they are really enemies of the cross of Christ. They are headed for destruction. Their god is their appetite, they brag about shameful things, and they think only about this life here on earth. *But we are citizens of heaven*" (Philippians 3:18-20 NLT).

Paul's warning concerns people who become "enemies of the cross of Christ" because they "think only about life here on earth." When we over-value our earthly citizenship, we under-value our heavenly citizenship. This sets us against God's priorities. As Christians, the ultimate leader of our lives is not some mortal human ruler or transient nation-state. Our leader is Jesus the King. And what a leader we have! Paul extols Jesus and the kingdom of which He has made us citizens:

**"We are citizens of heaven, where the Lord Jesus Christ lives."** Jesus ascended to heaven, and He exercises His power as Lord to advance His kingdom. He is not a self-absorbed human king who lives remotely from His subjects. He makes Himself personally accessible to help us as we serve Him. Jesus said, "I am with you always, even to the end of the age" (Matthew 28:20).

**"We are eagerly waiting for Him to return as our Savior."** Very soon, Jesus will return to establish His kingdom over all the earth. Just after Jesus ascended to heaven, His angels told His disciples, "This Jesus, who has been taken up from you into heaven, will come in just the same way as you have watched Him go into heaven" (Acts 1:11). We do not know exactly *when* He will return, but we know *that* He will return. The proper response to this fact is to "eagerly wait for Him," rather than getting inordinately consumed by earthly hopes—such as financial prosperity or political ideology.

**"He will take our weak mortal bodies and change them into**

**glorious bodies like His own."** When Jesus returns, He will give us eternal bodies like His. No more sickness, no more death, no more physical pain, no more unresolved sorrow (Revelation 21:4). No more doctor visits, no more health insurance premiums, no more funerals. Perfect physical health, perfect vitality, and expanded capacities. This will make our youthful health and vigor pale in comparison!

**"(He will use) the same power with which He will bring everything under His control."** When Jesus returns, He will establish His perfect kingdom over all the earth. He will exert His unlimited power to permanently defeat evil and to transform the earth so that it radiates the beauty and fruitfulness for which He created it. Think back to your most awesome experience with nature—and then multiply it by an infinite degree. The earth will be *filled* with the excellence, majesty, and beauty of the Lord! (Psalm 72:19)

How should we respond to these amazing promises? Paul does not leave us guessing. He writes, "Therefore, my dear brothers and sisters, stay true to the Lord." Don't let earthly goals and aspirations seduce you into forgetting that Jesus is your true and ultimate King. Don't let political loyalties usurp your loyalty to Jesus as your true Savior. Stay true to Him. Stand firm in His promises and stay faithful in your service to Him. Take heart from others, like Paul, who have lived this way (see Philippians 3:17). You will never regret it!

*Lord Jesus, thank You for being a Savior more amazing than I could have ever imagined. Thank You for saving me from the guilt of my many sins which would make me deserve Your righteous condemnation. Thank You for Your promise to return to complete the salvation You have already begun in me. Help me in the meantime, Lord, to stay true to You. Help me to stay on Your path and serve You today, and until I see You face to face.*

# 13

# ANXIOUS FOR NOTHING

**Philippians 4:5-7** Let your gentle spirit be known to all men. The Lord is near. Be anxious for nothing, but in everything by prayer and supplication with thanksgiving let your requests be made known to God. And the peace of God, which surpasses all comprehension, will guard your hearts and your minds in Christ Jesus.

---

In the course of an average day, how many times do you become annoyed or anxious? When I monitor my own heart, I discover that this usually happens *dozens* of times a day. My plans get interrupted, or a difficult person crosses my path. Annoyance quickly follows. It feels only natural to become anxious when a loved one makes a poor decision, or a concern about my health or finances arises in my mind.

I usually just repress these reactions and push ahead with my day—but these annoyances and anxieties tend to accumulate in my heart. Like a balloon filled with too much air, these emotions later come out sideways in a foul mood, a sense of self-pity, or touchiness toward others. More importantly, I find myself unable to show restraint and gentleness toward others, or to experience the peace of God guarding my heart and mind.

What is my problem? Why is my experience so different from

what this passage promises for me?

The answer is often embarrassingly simple: I forget that "the Lord is near." This statement is the promise upon which Paul's commands depend. The Lord is near. He is with me right now. He is not only *aware* of my annoyances and anxieties, but He is *accessible* for help as my loving Father. My mind affirms this statement, but my instinctive heart reaction is to live as an orphan—as if I am on my own to muddle through my annoyances and anxieties as best as I can.

What does it look like to respond differently to our daily annoyances and anxieties? How do we cash-in on this promise of God's accessibility so that gentleness replaces fearfulness—and peace replaces anxiety?

To begin, we can ask the Lord to sensitize us to the early outbreak of annoyance or anxiety. These reactions often happen on a subconscious level, and by the time we're aware of them they're usually already in charge of our hearts. This is why David prays, "Search me, O God, and know my heart; try me and know my anxious thoughts; and see if there be any hurtful way in me" (Psalm 139:23-24).

David provides keen insight: hurtful and anxious thoughts often ignite in our hearts *without our notice*. But the Lord is near, and He knows our heart better than we do. God can bring these thoughts to our conscious awareness. And the sooner we're aware that we're annoyed or anxious, the sooner we can take them to God.

In addition to being self-aware, we can go to God in prayer and simply pour our annoyances and anxieties out to Him—like a young child who runs to his mother and pours out his troubles. The Bible calls this kind of prayer "supplication." This refers to pouring out our annoyances and anxieties by communicating them to God in a raw, unvarnished way. Paul urges this in Philippians 4:6 ("with supplication"), and the Psalms contain hundreds of examples of supplication just like this. Here's one that speaks to me on a regular basis:

> Give ear to my prayer, O God; and do not hide Yourself from my *supplication*... I am restless in my complaint and am surely distracted, because of the voice of the enemy, because of the pressure of the wicked; for they bring down trouble upon me and in anger they bear a grudge against me. My heart is in anguish within me, and the terrors of death have fallen upon me. Fear and trembling come upon me (Psalm 55:1-5).

David's "supplication" leads him to pour out his restlessness, his complaints, and his deepest fears. Later, David recommends this kind of prayer to his hearers: "Cast your burden upon the Lord and He will sustain you" (Psalm 55:22). Deliberate supplication begins to transfer the burden of our annoyances and anxieties to the One who can both bear them and sustain us.

This sort of supplication leads naturally to petition—asking the Lord who is near for help with our annoyances and anxieties. Paul writes, "Let your requests be made known to God" (Philippians 4:6). God is accessible at this very moment. Right now, what help do you need God to give you? Why do you resist asking for this help? The psalmists often ask God to deliver them from their enemies, and to restore their hope and joy in Him. Such simple, almost child-like requests! But Jesus says that we should come to Him just like this—just like children. And far better to ask the Lord who is near for this kind of help than to not ask. As James writes, "You do not have because you do not ask" (James 4:2).

Paul promises that God will guard our hearts with His peace when we turn to Him in this way. The psalmists delight to praise God for answering their supplications and petitions.

> I waited patiently for the Lord to help me, and He turned to me and heard my cry. He lifted me out of the pit of despair, out of the mud and the mire. He set my feet on solid ground and steadied me as I walked along. He has given me a new song to sing, a hymn of praise to our God. Many will see what He

has done and be amazed. They will put their trust in the Lord (Psalm 40:1-3).

What annoyances or anxieties are plaguing you today? What will you do with them? Will you ignore them or try to fix them on your own? Or will you take them to the Lord who is near, pour them out to Him, and ask Him for help?

---

*Lord Jesus, thank you that you are not a distant and remote God who doesn't care about the insecurities and anxieties of my life. No, you are near to me in my time of need. Thank you that I have access to you as a child that can run freely to his father or mother. Help me to transfer the burden of my anxieties onto you because you are the One who can truly carry them!*

# 14

# THE PEACE OF CHRIST

**Colossians 3:12-15** So, as those who have been chosen of God, holy and beloved, put on a heart of compassion, kindness, humility, gentleness and patience; bearing with one another, and forgiving each other, whoever has a complaint against anyone; just as the Lord forgave you, so also should you. Beyond all these things put on love, which is the perfect bond of unity. Let the peace of Christ rule in your hearts, to which indeed you were called in one body; and be thankful.

Many Christians fail to grasp what it means to "let the peace of Christ rule in your hearts." I was one of them. As a new Christian, I was told that this verse contains a valuable principle of determining God's guidance in our lives: Do not make any important decision until you have God's peace about it. Wait until you feel peace from God before you move forward.

There is some truth in this principle. Each of us has a conscience which often registers a warning to our souls when we are about to violate God's will. We should be alert and responsive to such warnings—not going down a path that condemns. After all, "whatever is not of faith is sin" (Romans 14:23). This is good advice for all of us!

But what about those times when you know that a certain decision is God's will—but it fills you with fear rather than peace? Should you wait until you feel peace, or should you take a scary step of faith because God's love and wisdom are trustworthy? This is God's plain counsel in many places in Scripture, such as:

> Trust in the Lord with all your heart and do not lean on your own understanding. In all your ways acknowledge Him, and He will make your paths straight. Do not be wise in your own eyes; fear the Lord and turn away from evil (Proverbs 3:5-7).

Look closer at Colossians 3:15. You'll find that it is not a *general* principle for discerning God's guidance with big decisions; rather it is a *specific* principle of gaining God's guidance in our *unity* with one another.

The immediate context is about unity between Christians, or as Paul calls it, "the perfect bond of unity" (3:14). The peace Paul speaks of isn't inner peace, but peace with other Christians. This is the type of peace that should rule in our hearts because we "were called in one body" (3:15). God has united us with other believers through our union with Christ, making us members of the body of Christ. So, as we relate to one another, Paul states that we should let this peace or unity act as our "spiritual umpire." This peace should make the final call. In other words, we should prayerfully ask ourselves: "What response in this situation will *enhance our unity* and *express the truth that we are members of the same body*?"

This interpretation is confirmed by Paul's parallel passage in Ephesians 4:

> Therefore I... implore you to walk in a manner worthy of the calling with which you have been called, with all humility and gentleness, with patience, showing tolerance for one another in love, being diligent to preserve the unity of the Spirit in the bond of peace. There is one body and one Spirit, just as also you were called in one hope of your calling; one Lord, one faith, one baptism, one God and Father of all who is over all and through

all and in all (Ephesians 4:1-6).

Notice the striking similarities between these two passages. Both contain reminders of our unity with other Christians (Colossians 3:14-15; Ephesians 4:4-6), and both remind us of the character qualities that help us to live out this unity (Colossians 3:12-13; Ephesians 4:2). So, Paul's command in Colossians 3:15 to "let the peace of Christ rule in your hearts" is very similar to his exhortation in Ephesians: To "be diligent to preserve the unity of the Spirit in the bond of peace" (Ephesians 4:3).

Enough interpretation—now we must turn to application. How many times each day is this verse relevant to us? The closer we are to fellow believers, the greater opportunities we have to build unity or promote disunity. We may feel that such reactions are natural—even inevitable. But we are not mere animals acting on instinct with no choice but to react—like a dog snapping when you step on its tail. We are human beings made in God's image. And now by God's grace, we are His beloved children. And not only that, but God has also given us His Holy Spirit. The Holy Spirit goes to war with our sinful nature that desperately wants to act based on what we feel, rather than what is true (Galatians 5:17). Just consider the following common examples:

- A brother or sister hurts you through an unkind action, or a cold or even nasty word. How will you respond? Will you harbor their offense, rehearsing it over and over again in your mind? Will you return coldness with coldness, snub with snub? Will you decide: "I didn't sign up for this!" and distance yourself from them? Or will you prayerfully exercise your choice to forgive them, as God in Christ has forgiven you? Will you let their offense go, or perhaps bring it up for their good—whichever the Lord directs you to do? Which response lets the peace of Christ rule in your heart?
- As you get to know a brother or sister in Christ, you inevitably become aware of certain idiosyncrasies that irritate you. She talks about herself too much. He boasts about his ministry. She tends to be relationally pushy

rather than humbly engaging. Over time, these besetting sins will weigh on you. When talking about them to other brothers and sisters, will you unnecessarily point out their deficiencies? Will you subtly write them off in your heart and distance yourself from them? Or will you choose to bear with them in genuine love? Will you actively remember that God bears daily with your idiosyncrasies, that He draws near to you despite your besetting sins, and that it is His kindness that leads us to repentance? Will you choose to recall their strengths and even point these out to encourage them? Which response lets the peace of Christ rule in your heart?

- Someone mentions another believing church or ministry. You are aware of problems and deficiencies in this group. Will you take this opportunity to needlessly air your criticisms, or will you do your best to affirm them as allies rather than enemies? Again, which response lets the peace of Christ rule in your heart?

You represent Jesus to the watching world—whether you like it or not. How you choose to respond in these everyday situations will either promote unity or create disunity. Our choice to respond with genuine love is an important part of demonstrating the reality of Jesus by those who claim to follow Him (John 13:34-35).

---

*Lord Jesus, thank You for your amazing compassion and patience and forbearance. Thank You also for providing me with brothers and sisters in Christ, friends who help me to grow in You and represent You to a lost and broken world. Remind me today, as I interact with each one of them, to let the peace of Christ rule in my heart.*

# 15

# BE FILLED WITH THE SPIRIT

**Ephesians 5:18-21** Do not get drunk with wine, for that is dissipation, but be filled with the Spirit, speaking to one another in psalms and hymns and spiritual songs, singing and making melody with your heart to the Lord; always giving thanks for all things in the name of our Lord Jesus Christ to God, even the Father; and being subject to one another out of reverence for Christ.

There is a reason why we call alcohol beverages "spirits." We imbibe a little wine with friends, and the alcohol acts like an invisible spirit that elevates our mood and enhances our enjoyment of one another. This is why the Bible refers to wine as God's gift that "gladdens human hearts" (Psalm 104:15 TNIV). But drinking too much alcohol—allowing it to take control of our faculties—has a destructive effect. Drunkenness distorts our judgment, inflames our lusts, and deadens our minds. The result? Many people say that this makes them confident. I wonder. When you're drunk, do you genuinely feel confident, or do you merely feel less inhibition? Does getting drunk make you feel relaxed, or does it just dull your senses until you don't feel much at all? Sadly, many heavy drinkers can't tell the difference.

What is the God-given replacement for drunkenness? Read the passage again: "Be filled with the Spirit." Being filled with the Spirit has an ecstatic effect on the believer. That's why it leads to "making melody in your heart" (Ephesians 5:19). When we allow the Holy Spirit to fill us, our core needs get fulfilled: love, joy, peace, patience, kindness, gentleness, faithfulness, and self-control (Galatians 5:22-23).

Being filled with the Spirit sounds nice, but how does this happen? Does the Spirit just fall upon us out of the blue? Is this something we pray for? Paul answers this question in verses 19-21. Here we find five ways to become filled with the Spirit: "speaking," "singing," "making melody," "giving thanks," and "being subject." These participles evidently explain Paul's command to "be filled."[7] That is, we will be filled with the Spirit as we choose to speak, sing, make melody, give thanks, and serve one another. We can distill these five participles into three central ways to allow God's Spirit to fill us with His life.

**1. God's Spirit fills us as we choose to praise God.** Again, Paul writes, "Be filled with the Spirit, (by) speaking to one another in psalms and hymns and spiritual songs." The participle "speaking to *one another*" can also be translated "speaking to *yourselves* in psalms and hymns and spiritual songs." In other words, we can choose to focus our attention on who God has revealed Himself to be, speaking these words to ourselves. This is the medicine that cures our negative feelings and gives perspective on our current negative circumstances.

This seems to be what Paul has in mind, because the rest of verse 19 restates this idea by saying: "singing and making melody with your heart to the Lord." We can utilize biblical songs as a way of personally praising God—especially for His love and goodness and mercy. Sometimes we praise Him aloud with one another; sometimes we praise Him silently in private communion.

Many people wonder, "Why don't I experience the power of the Holy Spirit?" If you don't spend regular time praising God, look no further! Praising God is a direct channel to the power of the Holy Spirit in your life! As we cultivate this posture of personal praise, God draws near to us and fills our hearts with His Spirit in response to our choice to praise Him.

2. **God's Spirit fills us as we choose to thank Him for His faithfulness and goodness.** Paul writes, "Be filled with the Spirit... (by) always giving thanks for all things in the name of our Lord Jesus Christ to God, even the Father." When we rehearse people's offenses or focus on disappointments—or when we indulge in complaint and self-pity—we poison our souls. But as God's beloved children through our union with Jesus, we have another option. Every good thing comes to us from Him (James 1:17). He has met all of our deepest spiritual needs (Ephesians 1:3). His love for us is far greater than our circumstances (Romans 8:35-39). And He is able to work through all things for our good (Romans 8:28).

Based on these wonderful promises, we can cultivate a disposition of thanksgiving to our Heavenly Father. We can begin each day by thanking Him that this is the day that He has made (Psalm 118:24). As we go through each day, we can thank Him for how His promises enable us to meet each challenge. And at the end of each day, we can review how He has helped us and thank him all the more (Psalm 63:6-8). What a wonderful way to begin and end each day—far better than regretting the day's difficulties and fretting over tomorrow's problems! The more we overflow with thankfulness (Colossians 2:7), the more His Spirit imparts His peace and hope and joy to our hearts (Romans 15:13).

3. **God's Spirit fills us as we choose to serve the people He has placed in our lives.** Paul writes, "Be filled with the Spirit... (by) being subject to one another out of reverence to Christ." Jesus began His public ministry by joining sinful people in being baptized by His close relative, John the Baptist. In this way Jesus announced that He had come to serve—to identify with us in our condition, and ultimately to give His life as a ransom for our sins

(Mark 10:45). When He willingly chose to become God's Servant, God's Spirit came upon Him to empower Him for this ministry (Matthew 3:15-17). Likewise, when we serve others in humility, the Holy Spirit enters our lives to meet the pressing needs that we lack.

Have you ever felt mildly depressed or tired right before spending time with believers during a time of fellowship? How did you feel when you chose to serve others that night? Paul says that if we live selfishly—demanding our rights at the expense of others—we grieve God's Spirit (Ephesians 4:30). But as we choose to serve, God's Spirit will fill us, just as He filled Jesus. This is when we experience God so closely. He will grant us personal affirmation that we are His beloved children (Romans 8:15-16); He will give us His love and compassion for people (Philippians 2:1-2); He will give us His wisdom to love others (James 1:5); and He will give us His power to persevere over the long haul (Colossians 1:28-29). As often as we align ourselves with the Spirit's purpose to serve people, we can be sure that He will fill us in all of these ways, and surely many more.

---

*Lord Jesus, thank You for sending Your Spirit to fill me so that I may live like You lived—full of Your Father's peace, hope, and joy. Remind me to be filled with Your Spirit by humbly praising and thanking You, and by serving others in selfless love.*

# 16

# FIGHT THE GOOD FIGHT

**1 Timothy 1:18-19** This command I entrust to you, Timothy, my son, in accordance with the prophecies previously made concerning you, that by them you may fight the good fight, keeping faith and a good conscience, which some have rejected and suffered shipwreck in regard to their faith.

Have you ever watched a 12-round boxing match? Have you ever run a marathon? The New Testament uses both of these images to describe the Christian life. The Christian life begins with a simple decision to receive Jesus Christ and His free gift of forgiveness. And that simple decision guarantees that your eternal destiny with Jesus is secure. But the period between receiving Jesus and meeting Jesus is a long run and a grueling fight. Sadly, many do not finish. This is why there are so many New Testament passages that teach how to run the race, how to fight the good fight.

Paul commissioned Timothy to stay indefinitely in Ephesus in order to restore a church that had been ravaged by false teachers. Some of those false teachers may have even been elders of this church (Acts 20:29-30). So, you can imagine the mistrust and discouragement that Timothy was facing. He was facing a long haul in the days ahead—a fight.

So, in this letter Paul not only instructs Timothy on what to do; he also instructs him on how to stay in the fight. His instruction can help us to fight the good fight that God has assigned to each of us.

Paul's first instruction relates to "the prophecies previously made concerning you." Paul explicitly says that "by them" (referring to these prophecies) Timothy will be able to fight the good fight. He refers to these prophecies in two other places (1 Timothy 4:14 and 2 Timothy 1:6). So, they must have been important. The prophecies concerned a spiritual gift that would enable Timothy to play his role as Paul's colleague. To paraphrase Paul, "If you remember how God has gifted you and faithfully use that gift, this will help you to fight the good fight."

"That sounds like it would be encouraging for Timothy," you might say, "but not for an average Christian like me." Not true! The New Testament teaches that God has given all Christians at least one spiritual gift (1 Corinthians 12:11; Romans 12:6). As we choose to serve God in community with other Christians, He will reveal how He has gifted us to make a special contribution to His church. Although we may not receive a prophecy identifying our gift, we will usually receive a pattern of feedback from other Christians that confirms our gifts. The God who gifts us to serve Him certainly knows best how to communicate what gifts He has given us.

But the question remains: How does faithfully using our spiritual gifts help us to persist in fighting the good fight?

For one, we fight most effectively when we use the equipment God gave us. In real warfare, would you rather fight with a rifle or a peashooter? When we use our spiritual gifts, God uses us to make a unique contribution to God's kingdom—one that He designed us to make. Are you gifted in teaching? Encouragement? Counseling? Serving? When you activate your gifts, you will gain a direct experience of God's empowerment. Peter writes, "Do you have the gift of speaking? Then speak as though God himself were speaking through you. Do you have the gift of helping others?

Do it with all the strength and energy that God supplies" (1 Peter 4:11).

In addition, a direct connection exists between our use of our spiritual gifts and our motivation to serve God. It feels good to use our gifts. God brings happiness into our lives when we use them to build up others. This motivation helps us to persevere through times of difficulty, discouragement, and even spiritual attack. This is why Christians who know how they're gifted and who faithfully use their gifts are more likely to stay in the fight over many years.

Do you know how God has gifted you to serve Him? If not, ask Him to reveal this to you as you serve others with your brothers and sisters in Christ. If you do know, find ways to use your gifts on a regular basis—and this will greatly help you to fight the good fight.

Spiritual gifts are not enough to fight the good fight. Paul gives a second instruction: "Keep a good conscience." A good conscience refers to being sensitive and responsive to God's personal moral guidance. God has given every human being a moral compass. To function properly, this conscience must be renewed by God's Holy Spirit and trained by His Word. As we walk with God, He will use our conscience to warn us of impending moral danger, and He will correct us when we deviate from His moral guidance. None of us live morally perfect lives. But it is of the utmost importance that we regularly respond to God's conviction through our conscience (see 2 Corinthians 1:12; 1 Timothy 1:5). This is the lesson God impressed upon David after He restored him from his affair with Bathsheba:

> I will instruct you and teach you in the way which you should go; I will counsel you with My eye upon you. Do not be as the horse or as the mule which have no understanding, whose trappings include bit and bridle to hold them in check, otherwise they will not come near to you. Many are the sorrows of the wicked, but he who trusts in the Lord, lovingkindness shall surround him (Psalm 32:8-10).

Are you a "moral mule"? To be a "moral mule" is to reject a good conscience, and to plunge your life into moral chaos and personal misery.

- Do you listen to counsel from God and wise Christians around you? Or do you surround yourself with people who affirm everything you do?
- How many times does God need to convict your heart about a sinful pattern in your life before you respond to him?
- Do you normally heed God's warnings of moral danger, or do you normally reserve the right to disregard them?
- Do you respond quickly to God's moral correction, or do you normally minimize your problem or blame-shift?

To be sensitive to God's moral counsel is to keep a good conscience, to trust His moral guidance, and to live with the protection of His lovingkindness. All of this is the difference between keeping or rejecting a good conscience, and a good conscience is an indispensable element in fighting the good fight!

---

*Lord Jesus, thank You for forgiving all of my sins and promising me eternal life. And thank You for giving me a good fight to fight until I see You face to face. I am not able to fight this good fight without Your empowerment and protection. Thank You for promising to be with me every step of the way. Help me to faithfully use the spiritual gifts You have given me, and teach me to keep a good conscience as I walk with You. Surround me with Your lovingkindness.*

# 17

# THE FEAR OF DEATH

**Hebrews 2:14-17 NLT** Because God's children are human beings—made of flesh and blood—the Son also became flesh and blood. For only as a human being could He die, and only by dying could He break the power of the devil, who had the power of death. Only in this way could He set free all who have lived their lives as slaves to the fear of dying… It was necessary for Him to be made in every respect like us… so that He could be our merciful and faithful High Priest before God. Then He could offer a sacrifice that would take away the sins of the people.

Even very young people sometimes experience terror at the prospect of death. As we advance in age, our bodies remind us (in many ways!) of our mortality. This fear can dominate our field of vision and make us terrified or despondent. What answer does the God of the Bible give us to this universal problem?

Humans have an instinctive sense that death is abnormal. The Bible rejects the view that human death is natural. It is not "the final stage of growth," as one secular author calls it.[8] No, God created us to live forever. Satan holds "the power of death," and he uses our fear of dying to make us slaves. This enslavement takes different cultural forms.

In animistic cultures, people live in fear of angering the spirits that control their lives. When I visited southeast Asia some years ago, a human stampede on a crowded bridge resulted in hundreds of deaths. The next day, shrines with fruit sacrifices sprang up all over the city—erected by poor people who were terrified. When I asked about the sacrifices, I was told that this was their attempt to appease the angry spirits so that they would not kill the worshippers. How many billions of people live in this kind of daily bondage to the fear of death?

In cultures dominated by reincarnation, people live in fear of being punished in the next life for their failure to live up to religious law in this life. Serious-minded religionists believe (correctly) that the purpose of this life is to prepare for their next life—being blessed by God. But they also believe (incorrectly) that the only way to qualify for God's blessing is by obeying religious laws. But how much obedience is required? How good is good enough? For many, this question gnaws at the conscience of millions, inducing a growing fear of judgment. For others, self-righteous denial dulls their conscience.

In secular cultures like our own, people have less fear of divine judgment because they don't believe in God or the afterlife. Yet the certainty of their own deaths casts a terrible shadow over their lives. As an atheist in my teen years, I vividly remember the terrifying realization that my life had no ultimate meaning. I was going to die. I was going to cease to know that I had ever existed. All of my loved ones would suffer the same fate. The sun would eventually burn out, and all evidence of our existence would be erased. In view of such an obvious and awful fact, how could I live the rest of my life without succumbing to despair? This is why secular people are often enslaved to distraction: the next purchase, the next form of entertainment, the next career advancement, or the next romantic relationship. These provide the illusion of meaning and hope. Or at the very least, they distract us from the meaninglessness of our secular lives.

What is God's solution to our fear of death? Jesus entered into our mortal condition and conquered the root of the problem. He took on our humanity and lived in this death-dominated world. He died a representative death. He voluntarily gave up His perfect life as an atoning sacrifice for our sins. His righteous death satisfied God's justice, forever silencing Satan's accusation that we must be condemned to eternal death for our sins. His resurrection demonstrated His conquest of sin and death. The way to eternal life is now open to all who personally entrust themselves to Jesus as their Savior. Thus, John 3:16 declares that "God so loved the world that He gave His one and only Son, that *whoever believes in Him* might not perish, but have eternal life."

Having been delivered from the power of death, we who believe in Jesus can also be freed from the fear of death to live meaningful lives. I vividly remember the joyous sense of freedom I experienced as a new Christian in this regard. I was actually going to live forever with God! This fact put all of my fears and problems in a new and profoundly hopeful light. Even now, over fifty years later, as a I face a life-threatening illness, I am strengthened and stabilized by the assurance that God will be with me forever: "The *eternal* God is a refuge, and underneath are the *everlasting* arms" (Deuteronomy 33:27).

---

*Lord Jesus, thank You for entering into this death-dominated human condition. Thank You for delivering me from the power of death through Your own death. I cannot begin to fathom how great this sacrifice was for You. I will never understand how great Your love must be to voluntarily die for such a sinful person as me. I rejoice that I will live forever with You and Your people. Help me to live the remainder of this life as a light who draws others to You.*

# 18

# RUNNING THE RACE

**Hebrews 12:1-3** Therefore, since we have so great a cloud of witnesses surrounding us, let us also lay aside every encumbrance and the sin which so easily entangles us, and let us run with endurance the race that is set before us, fixing our eyes on Jesus, the author and perfecter of faith, who for the joy set before Him endured the cross, despising the shame, and has sat down at the right hand of the throne of God. For consider Him who has endured such hostility by sinners against Himself, so that you will not grow weary and lose heart.

The Christian life is a long journey. It begins the moment that we entrust ourselves to Jesus as our Savior, and it continues until we die, or He returns. It is a marathon, not a sprint. It is for plodding tortoises, not for sprinting hares.

This is why the author of Hebrews emphasizes endurance. He uses this word four times in the first seven verses of Hebrews 12. He describes its antithesis as "growing weary and losing heart" (v.3). Endurance is not flashy, and it is not a popular concept in our quick-fix, convenience-obsessed culture. But nonetheless, it is an essential aspect of Christian spirituality.

One reason for its necessity is that we, like the original recipients of this letter, live in a spiritually antagonistic environment. These first-century Christians faced public shame, material dispossession, imprisonment, and even death. This has been the norm—not the exception—for most Christians over the past 2,000 years. For many reasons, Christians in the West have been spared these threats—but this is truly an abnormal period in history. And it may be coming to a close. Regardless, as Paul says elsewhere, "*All* who desire to live godly in Christ Jesus will be persecuted" (2 Timothy 3:12). If you commit yourself to live the rest of your life for Christ, you will experience various forms of spiritual opposition all along the way. Are you ready to face spiritual opposition? Have you made up your mind in advance to stand for Christ? How can you cultivate this endurance? These three verses supply us with three helpful insights.

**1. "Therefore, since we have so great a cloud of witnesses surrounding us… let us run with endurance the race set before us."** This "great cloud of witnesses" refers to the Old Testament believers described in the previous chapter (Hebrews 11). God had set a race before each of them—and they had run it with endurance. Not perfectly. Not without slips and falls and periods of frustration and fear and discouragement. But they played their roles in God's great plan before they passed on.

They are "witnesses," not in the sense that they are watching us and witnessing how we're running (though they may indeed be doing this). Rather, they are witnesses in the sense that their lives testify to us that it is possible to run the race with endurance. Briefly read about their lives in chapter 11 of Hebrews, and you will find that God supplied them with everything they needed for their races. They supplied only one thing: imperfect faith. This was enough for God. And it is enough for our lives as well.

God has supplied us with many more witnesses in the past 2,000 years—from the famous Christian leaders recorded in the New Testament right up to those lesser-known brothers and sisters He has put in your life today. From all of them, we can learn about the foundational importance of God's faithfulness. From all of them, we can learn valuable lessons about trusting God over the long haul. Are you losing endurance? Learn their stories so that they can encourage you to keep running your race!

**2. "Let us also lay aside every encumbrance and the sin which so easily entangles us, and let us run with endurance the race set before us."** Imagine trying to run a marathon while carrying two heavy suitcases. Your arms, legs, and back would never forgive you! Sooner or later, you would have to choose between laying aside your suitcases and getting on with your race.

Surely our author is not suggesting that we must become sinless in order to live the Christian life! He would be contradicting the entire Bible (see for example James 3:1 and 1 John 1:8)—let alone his own letter (see the sinful characters in chapter 11)!

What exactly is he saying then? From time to time, God will show you something current and specific that is incompatible with following Him. Are you willing to lay it aside with His help? It may be an unwillingness to forgive an offender. It may be an unhealthy romantic relationship. It may be an inordinate love for a hobby. Whatever it is, don't justify it. Don't tighten your grip around it. Don't tell yourself that you are unable to let go of it. Just agree with God that it is a hindrance, and take the step He shows you to let it go. He will break its power over you, and you will be glad as you run with greater freedom.

**3. "Let us run with endurance the race that is set before us, fixing our eyes on Jesus, the author and perfecter of faith, who for the joy set before Him endured the cross, despising the shame, and has sat down at the right hand of the throne of God. For consider Him… so that you will not grow weary and lose heart."** Of all the people who have run their races before us, no one is greater than Jesus. This is why we are told to "fix our eyes" on Him, and to "consider Him." Both words emphasize carefully focusing on Him.

Jesus is "the Author and Perfecter of faith." This means, for one thing, that He is the ultimate Example of what it looks like to run the race with endurance. No one has ever had a more difficult race to run. Yet, He ran it all the way through—from the shameful cross to His Father's throne. He kept going because He knew that the joy of finishing would be well worth it. If Jesus ran His great race for us, this will motivate us to run our races for Him.

But Jesus is not just our ultimate Example; He is also our ever-present Helper. He is with us, and He will mature our faith as we ask Him to help us keep running. This is how the author describes Him earlier in his letter: "For we do not have a high priest who cannot sympathize with our weaknesses, but One who has been tempted in all things as we are, yet without sin. Therefore let us draw near with confidence to the throne of grace, so that we may receive mercy and find grace to help in time of need" (Hebrews 4:15).

---

*Lord Jesus, thank You for running Your great race for me. Thank You for all of the witnesses that encourage me to run my race with endurance. Thank You most of all for running my race with me. Help me this day to run this part of my race.*

# 19

# DIVINE DISCIPLINE

**Hebrews 12:4-11 NIV** In your struggle against sin, you have not yet resisted to the point of shedding your blood. And have you completely forgotten this word of encouragement that addresses you as a father addresses his son? It says, "My son, do not make light of the Lord's discipline, and do not lose heart when He rebukes you, because the Lord disciplines the one He loves, and He chastens everyone He accepts as His son." Endure hardship as discipline; God is treating you as His children. For what children are not disciplined by their father? If you are not disciplined—and everyone undergoes discipline—then you are not legitimate, not true sons and daughters at all. Moreover, we have all had human fathers who disciplined us and we respected them for it. How much more should we submit to the Father of spirits and live! They disciplined us for a little while as they thought best; but God disciplines us for our good, in order that we may share in His holiness. No discipline seems pleasant at the time, but painful. Later on, however, it produces a harvest of righteousness and peace for those who have been trained by it.

Why do some people "run with endurance the race" set before them, while others do not? (Hebrews 12:1).

God has placed before each of His children a unique race to run, a unique role in His plan to play. Since this race is a marathon, we shall need "endurance" (used 5 times in 12:1-13). And endurance is the result of much training—which is what the word "discipline" means (a term used 10 times in this passage).

We usually think of discipline as reactive correction. The Greek word for "discipline" (*paideia*) does include this sort of correction. However, it primarily refers to proactive training. Just as a trainer subjects an athlete to a variety of rigorous exercises, God subjects His children to a variety of hardships so that we will develop the endurance that is necessary to finish our races, and these "tribulations bring about perseverance" (Romans 5:3). Only God knows how long and steep our race will be. So, He serves as the perfect leader of our lives who takes us through hardships so that we will persevere to the end.

God is all-wise. Thus, He knows how much endurance we need, and He knows what types of hardships will best develop this endurance.

God is also sovereign. He is in charge of the universe in general, and everything in it. Therefore, He can train us even through hardships that He did not initiate. Joseph's brothers threw him in a pit and sold him into slavery. But at the end of his life, Joseph could say to his abusive brothers: "You meant it as evil, but God meant it for good" (Genesis 50:20).

The recipients of this letter were experiencing persecution for their faith in Jesus (Hebrews 10:32-36; 12:3-4). Free moral agents inflicted this persecution on these believers—not God. Yet the author insists that God is working through this persecution to train them to run with endurance. Thus, he says: "Endure (every) hardship as discipline" (Hebrews 12:7). Truly, all of our hardships—even those inflicted on us unjustly by evil people and Satan—are allowed and used by God to train us to fulfill His purpose for our lives.

Many years ago, I went through a series of very painful hardships.

Each time these hardships seemed about to go away, they resumed with even greater intensity. When my wife phoned me to tell me that another hardship had been prolonged, I protested: "It feels like God is helping me to my feet—only to sucker-punch me again. I don't know what I'm supposed to be learning."

There was a long silence, and then she said: "What if God is getting you ready for even more difficult hardships that you'll need to endure in the future?" I was speechless—and disappointed—by her question. Yet her words rang in my ears long after I hung up. I knew she had spoken a truth that I needed to hear. And I have lived to be grateful for the endurance that this period of special training developed.

The author notes that his audience has "completely forgotten" this aspect of God's fatherly love (Hebrews 12:4). We are the same way. When we face even moderate hardship, we easily forget this precious truth. God knows what training we need, and He loves us enough to administer it. Yet how easily we question His wisdom, accuse Him of not caring about us, and threaten to quit running unless He removes the very training we need. God takes no joy in our suffering, but He encourages us to remember that His discipline is a profound proof of His love.

How do we thrive during times of God's discipline? We need to focus on His promises—especially those named in this passage. Three promises stand out as especially important.

**1. "We have all had human fathers who disciplined us and we respected them for it. How much more should we submit to the Father of spirits and live!"** The author draws a contrast between our earthly parents (literally, "fathers of our flesh") and God ("the Father of our spirits"). If we respected our parents' effort to train us in rudimentary life-skills, certainly we should respect God's wise training which enables us to flourish as spiritual beings.

**2. "[Our human fathers] disciplined us for a little while as they thought best; but God disciplines us for our good, in order that**

**we may share in His holiness."** God's holiness refers to His moral character. He is loving, kind, upright, and wise. Since He created us in His image, we were designed to make the unique beauty of His character visible in this world. His discipline is thus always aimed at securing our ultimate good, our true happiness.

**3. "No discipline seems pleasant at the time, but painful. Later on, however, it produces a harvest of righteousness and peace for those who have been trained by it."** No one has ever regretted cooperating with God's training, because it always leads to eventual flourishing that far outweighs its painfulness at the time. God's discipline leads to compounding and cumulative effects. Here we find the secret to thriving during times of God's discipline. Do not focus on the present pain; focus on the future harvest!

---

*Lord Jesus, thank You for submitting to much painful discipline so that You could qualify to be our Savior. Although You despised the shame inflicted upon You by evil people, You looked forward to the joy of securing many children for Your Father. Teach me to trust in Your wisdom and goodness as You train me to run my race with endurance.*

# 20

# DON'T QUIT

**Hebrews 12:12** Therefore, strengthen the hands that are weak and the knees that are feeble, and make straight paths for your feet, so that the limb which is lame may not be put out of joint, but rather be healed.

Hebrews 12 begins with the exhortation: "Let us run with endurance the race set before us" (12:1). It concludes with a similar exhortation to keep on running despite weariness and injury.

The Christian life is like a long-distance race. There will be times when we "hit the wall," and feel sorely tempted to quit. But we have ample resources with which to renew our strength—if we draw upon them. The "therefore" that begins this passage points us back to the resources previously described in chapter 12:

- Earlier believers, who have completed their races, can provide us with inspiration and insight to run our races (12:1a).
- Jesus—who is not only our ultimate Example, but also our ever-present Helper—will be with us every step of the way (12:2-3).
- Our Heavenly Father is training us through hardships, developing in us the endurance we need to get to the finish line (12:4-11).

Drawing upon these resources, we are to renew our decision before God to stay in the race to which He has assigned us. This is what it means to "strengthen the hands that are weak, and the knees that are feeble," and to "make straight paths for your feet." Picture a marathon runner who is exhausted and staggering off-course, looking for any excuse to quit. To persevere until the end, he needs to remember the next milestone in the race, his friends and family who have come to cheer him on, and the forthcoming finish line. Such reminders are needed to re-energize him to finish the race. Such is the imagery of this passage.

But what does it look like specifically to recommit yourself to the race that God has set before you? Many related truths have been helpful to me over the years.

**Do you need to turn away from self-pity?** Ask God to help you to replace this terribly debilitating mindset with gratitude. Thank Him for the privilege of having a race to run, and for all of the help He provides. And while you're at it, reject the urge to envy other runners who are in a season of current ease and good fortune. Instead, affirm that God has selected both the race and the training that is best for you.

**Are you worrying about the challenges that might lie further down the road?** What good is that going to do? Focus instead on being faithful to God for this one day. God will not supply us today with help for tomorrow's possible needs. But He will meet us with all the help we need to run today's course. What does God want you to do today? What step can you take today in that direction?

**Are you focused on regret for your past failures?** The older we get, the more potential regrets we accumulate, and the more tempting it is to live in those regrets. Alternatively, nostalgia can commandeer our mental focus, getting us to think about the bygone "good old days." Yet, both regret and nostalgia will hinder you from the tasks God has put before you *today*. This is why Paul tells us to deliberately "forget" what lies behind and to "press on" toward what lies ahead (Philippians 3:13-14). Remember that God forgives you for past failures, and that He can work through them to grow your appreciation of His grace. Remember also that He has great blessings in store for you in the future—so run toward them!

**Are you using your current "lameness" as an excuse to drop out of the race?** Imagine writing this sentence on a piece of paper: "I can't run the race God set before me because of _____." How would you fill in the blank? Or what are you filling in the blank that is keeping you from running the race?

Circumstantial adversities, emotional pain, and declining health make it easier to believe the lie that our race is over. In physical races, injuries do indeed force us to the sidelines until we recover. But in this race, the author says: "Make straight paths for your feet, *so that* the limb which is lame may not be put out of joint, but rather be healed." In other words, it is as we run (while still lame!) that we experience healing. If you are willing to limp forward, doing what you can to follow God, He will meet you with His recuperative power.

**Are you allowing yourself to be isolated from fellow Christian servants?** Depression drives us toward solitude and loneliness. But this kind of isolation only leads to increased negative thinking. For example, Elijah isolated himself after Jezebel's threat—and wound up wanting to die! (see 1 Kings 19:1-10) So, during times of depression, reject the urge to isolate, and "pursue righteousness, faith, love and peace *with* those who call upon the Lord with a pure heart" (2 Tim. 2:23). Tell a Christian friend about your weariness. Ask him for advice and encouragement. Pray with him for renewed energy. Then run alongside him as much as possible.

**One last piece of advice: An important part of running the race is encouraging other flagging runners.** That is what the author is doing in this passage (12:1-13). And earlier in his letter, he wrote, "Encourage one another day after day, as long as it is still called 'Today,' so that none of you will be hardened by the deceitfulness of sin" (Hebrews 3:13). Sin can deceive our hearts. We need this sort of encouragement "day after day" so that we do not quit the race, falling into discouragement. What a blessing it is to receive a pointed word of encouragement during these times. Who in your life needs this sort of encouragement?

---

*Thank You, Lord Jesus, for reminding me that the Christian life is a long-distance race. I need that reminder because I sometimes grow weary and am tempted to lose heart. Show me today how to resume the race You have set before me. Give me today the eyes to recognize fellow runners who need encouragement, and give me the words that will help them to keep going until they see You face to face.*

# 21

# THE PRAYER OF A RIGHTEOUS PERSON

**James 5:16-20 NIV** Therefore confess your sins to each other and pray for each other so that you may be healed. The prayer of a righteous person is powerful and effective. Elijah was a human being, even as we are. He prayed earnestly that it would not rain, and it did not rain on the land for three and a half years. Again he prayed, and the heavens gave rain, and the earth produced its crops. My brothers and sisters, if one of you should wander from the truth and someone should bring that person back, remember this: Whoever turns a sinner from the error of their way will save them from death and cover over a multitude of sins.

Most of us have friends and family members who have received Jesus, but who are currently not following Him. This is a special sort of heartache—often difficult to put into words. We know that the story isn't over for our loved ones, but what can we do to influence them to return to the Lord?

Prayer has a powerful impact on such people. James' encouraging words of turning people back to the Lord (verses 19-20) are immediately preceded by his exhortation to pray (verses 16-18). We can "turn them back" from a lifestyle of sin and error through our prayers for them. We pray for them "that [they] may be healed" (James 5:16).

James cites Elijah as an encouragement to pray in this way. Elijah was a "righteous person." However, this simply means that he was in right standing with God—just as we are in Christ (Romans 5:1). Elijah had his flaws—just like the rest of us. And he wrestled with great despair at times—just like the rest of us (see 1 Kings 19). But God used this "man with a nature like ours" to change the world through powerful prayer. He did this in a few ways.

First, Elijah prayed for drought to come upon Israel as a discipline for their waywardness. Elijah "prayed earnestly that it would not rain, and it did not rain on the earth for three years and six months" (NIV). As a prophet of God, Elijah knew God had warned Israel that He would discipline them through drought when they turned away from Him (Deuteronomy 28:15, 24). God therefore answered Elijah's prayers for drought. This created a crisis in Israel, but this painful predicament ultimately led many to see their need for God and turn back to Him in a dramatic way (1 Kings 18:39).

Are you willing to pray for your wayward loved ones that God will discipline them—through painful hardship if need be—so that they might soften their hearts? This is certainly not a popular idea in our culture, but it is a biblical one. How grateful many of us are that Christians were praying for us along these lines when we were far from God! It is worth it to experience hardship, if that experience influences us to come to our senses and turn back to God.

Second, Elijah prayed for God to bless Israel as soon as they began to show signs of repentance. James writes, "Then he prayed again, and the sky poured rain and the earth produced its fruit" (NIV). Immediately after he saw some of Israel's leaders turn back to God, Elijah prayed for the drought to end, and God answered his prayer with a heavy shower (1 Kings 18:41-44). How consistent God's answer was with His character! He disciplines us for our good, and He is merciful when we turn back to Him. He loves to bless His people at the first sign of our willingness to trust Him!

We can pray in a similar way for our wayward loved ones. Having prayed for God's discipline when they were stubbornly resistant, we can also pray for God's blessing when they show the first signs of turning back to Him. Their wayward years may have deceived them into fearing God as an exacting taskmaster. But our prayers for God's blessing when they begin to repent can help them to regain a renewed view of God. What a privilege to partner with God in this way!

Finally, Elijah prayed for wayward Israel for several years. Some of us have prayed for wayward loved ones for many years too. Such prayer takes time. Perseverance is unavoidable. But prayers of this kind are uniquely effective. Ajith Fernando writes:

> Praying is the most powerful thing we do on earth. Let us be faithful at it… It may be prayer for the repentance of a child or of a fellow Christian under the grip of Satan. [Such] people may not be open to listen to us when we advise them… But we can take the battle to a higher plane. We can fight Satan, who holds them in his grip, so that the grip will be loosened and they will be less resistant to the wooing of God's Spirit.[9]

Continue to persevere in prayer. If you feel doubts about praying today, claim God's promise that your prayers are unleashing His powerful influence into the lives of your loved ones.

*Thank You, Lord Jesus, for allowing me to partner with You through prayer for my wayward loved ones. I know that You will not violate their free will, but I also know that Your influence is far greater than mine. Help me to love them enough to pray for their discipline when they are stubborn. And help me to pray in faith for their blessing at the first sign of their repentance. Thank You that the day is coming when You will show me all of the ways that You have answered these prayers. In the meantime, help me to persevere in loving them in this way.*

# 22

# LOVE COVERS OVER A MULTITUDE OF SINS

**Proverbs 10:12** Hatred stirs up strife, but love covers all transgressions.

**James 5:20** He who turns a sinner from the error of his way will save his soul from death and will cover a multitude of sins.

**1 Peter 4:8** Above all, keep fervent in your love for one another, because love covers a multitude of sins.

---

What does the Bible mean when it says that our love for others covers a multitude of sins?

We can begin to answer this question by noting what this statement does *not* mean, according to other biblical passages.

- It does not mean that our love atones—or pays the penalty—for others' sins. Only God's love, expressed through Jesus' death on the cross, can pay for human sins. As John writes, "If anyone sins, we have an Advocate with the Father, Jesus Christ the righteous, and He Himself is the atoning sacrifice for our sins" (1 John 2:1-2).
- It does not mean that love always conceals others' sins. Hiding a father's chronic abuse of his wife and children,

for example, is not Christian love. Such immoral behavior should be exposed so that the father might repent, and his family might have a chance to heal and flourish. This is why Paul says, "Do not participate in the unfruitful deeds of darkness, but instead even expose them" (Ephesians 5:11).

When we look closely at each of these three passages, we discover that they each apply this maxim in a different way.

**"Hatred stirs up strife, but love covers all transgressions" (Proverbs 10:12).** Here, Solomon contrasts how hatred and love respond to someone's sinful acts. "Hatred stirs up strife," presumably by delighting to tell others about the sin. Hatred asks, "How can I use this information to hurt the offender, or to impress others that I am in the know?" Like gasoline on a fire, such gossip only inflames and ignites the damage of the original sin. Love, however, is discreet with such information. It "covers" such sin by not telling others about it unless doing so is necessary. Love asks, "Is there a good reason why someone else should know about this? If not, I will keep it to myself."

**"He who turns a sinner from the error of his way will save his soul from death and will cover a multitude of sins" (James 5:20).** James is referring in context to a fellow Christian who has turned away from God and His truth (James 5:19). How should we respond to this situation? We might respond vindictively: "I hope he gets what he deserves!" Or we might respond apathetically: "Oh well, she has chosen to go down that path. There's nothing I can do." Is this love? Surely not. Such responses are uncaring, and overlook the possibility of having a redemptive influence on our straying brother or sister. We can certainly pray for God's loving discipline, as Elijah prayed when Israel was straying from God (James 5:17). As we pray for wayward friends, God might change our hearts in the process. During extended times of prayer, God will lead us to plead with them to return to Him, or to show them a special kindness. If we cooperate with God in these ways, they might turn back to God. Then we will have "covered a multitude of sins." That is, by influencing them toward repentance, we will have helped to rescue them from further ruin and sorrow.

**"Above all, keep fervent in your love for one another, because love covers a multitude of sins" (1 Peter 4:8).** Why is ongoing, sincere, intentional love for our brothers and sisters so important? One answer, according to Peter, is this: "Because love covers a multitude of sins." Peter recognizes that because Christians are sinners, our churches are bound to be full of all kinds of sins. Not only overt sins like drunkenness and sexual immorality and anger outbursts, but also covert sins like jealousy and resentment and relational apathy (see for example Galatians 5:19-21).

How can we combat these sins? How can we minimize the damage they cause? Not by simply resisting them or correcting them (though this is often necessary). The main way we "cover" these sins in our relationships is to prioritize intentionally loving one another.

Suppose my home church friend has a bad habit of speaking insensitively. I think, "His insensitivity is hurtful and offensive. I will try to get him to stop this bad habit." I bring up his insensitivity, and he agrees it is a problem—but he remains pretty insensitive. The more I focus on this shortcoming, the more annoyed I become. Annoyance gives birth to resentment, and I begin to withdraw from the relationship. What a mess!

What if instead of focusing on his flaws, I choose to focus on his strengths? I keep a new list—not of the times he has been insensitive, but of how he has grown in other areas: how he is loyal to God's truth, and how he is willing to speak up on important matters. His insensitivity remains, but now I see it in a more accurate context. Now I can bear his insensitivity more easily. Why? Because I choose to see him in his entirety—not partially—focusing on his strengths as well as his sins. Then, a miracle happens when I begin to encourage him in his strengths, express gratitude for our friendship, and praise his strengths to others. His sin is still there, but it no longer defines him in my eyes or dominates our relationship. Active love has "covered" his sin. As one theologian writes:

> Where love abounds in a fellowship of Christians, many small offences, and even some large ones, are readily overlooked and forgotten. But where love is lacking, every word is viewed with suspicion, every action is liable to misunderstanding, and conflicts abound—to Satan's perverse delight."[10]

---

*Lord Jesus, thank You for not only paying the penalty for my sins through Your death, but also for covering my many sins by Your steadfast love. You don't define me by my sins. You view me as a beloved child of God. You correct me when necessary, but You always encourage me and have a positive vision for my life. Help me to love my brothers and sisters in the same way.*

# 23

# WHY DOES GOD LOVE ME?

**1 John 4:8, 10** God is love… This is real love—not that we loved God, but that He loved us and sent His Son as a sacrifice to take away our sins.

Why does God love you? Such a simple question. But one that we often misunderstand.

Deep in our fallen hearts lies the belief that God loves us because there is something lovable within us. After all, that's the way we love: We love because we find people and things lovable. We say, "I love strawberry ice cream *because* of its flavor" or "I love you *because* you have such a great personality." We love *because* there is something lovable in the person or object.

But is this the reason God loves you?

Read again what John says: "This is real love—*not* that we loved Him but that He loved us." Did you catch that? God does not love us because of our great love for Him. God loves us because it is His essential nature to love. God's love for us is always prior to our love for Him. Paul says that "while we were yet helpless… ungodly…

sinners... enemies," God loved us and sent His Son Jesus to die for us so that we might be reconciled to Him (Romans 5:6-10). This is why C. S. Lewis said, "God did not die for [us] because of some value He perceived in [us]... He loved us not because we were lovable, but because He is love."[11] Any love we have for God is only a response to this prior and foundational love that He has for us.

We might brush this off as abstract theology that offers no impact on our lives. But not so fast. If we assume God's love depends on our love for him, we make a mistake that is bound to injure us. All seems to go well when we perform well, but when our deficiencies appear, or we have a moral fall—what then? Our reflex might be to deny or minimize our shortfalls. Desperately, we might even tell ourselves, "Yes, but there are these good things in me that God values." But such thinking is profoundly mistaken. It puts our relationship with God on a very shaky foundation: the love of God depends on how well we've been performing lately.

Some Christians emphasize that God loves us because of our great faith in Him. Not true. God loved us and wanted to bless us long before we ever believed in Him. Our faith in God is important, but *not* because it inclines God to bless us. Instead, our faith enables us to receive and enjoy the blessing that God is already inclined to give us—for reasons we will never fully fathom. It's like the old song says:

> I don't know why Jesus loved me.
> I don't know why He cared.
> I don't know why He sacrificed His life,
> Oh, but I'm glad, so glad He did.

Such a love brings both humility and confidence into my heart. It humbles me because I know my moral performance and comparison to others is not the grounds for God's love for me. It humbles me to know God loves me in spite of my many sins against Him—even despite my daily aversion toward Him. But knowing God loves me because it is His nature to love also gives me great confidence before Him. I don't have to shrink from Him when my sins spring to the surface. He knew they were there all along, and He loved me anyhow. Even in the middle of a moral fall, I can come to Him boldly and with confidence because He is loving and because He has sent His Son to pay for all of my many sins.

Writing on this same topic, William R. Newell put it this way: "To consent to be loved by God… and to expect to be blessed by God, while realizing all the more our unworthiness—that is the great secret."[12] This glorious truth is indeed a "great secret"—not because God hides it from us, but because it is so counterintuitive to our way of thinking. Right now, ask God to teach you to think this way about His love, and His instruction will transform your life!

---

*Lord Jesus, thank You for pursuing me with Your unconditional and steadfast love. It is my pride that wants to deserve Your love. It is my pride that wants You to love me because of how much I do for You, because of how much I love You, and because of how strong my faith in You is. Thank You for revealing that You love me because of who You are, not because of who I am or what I do. May my many failures teach me child-like dependence on Your love, instead of dependence on my self-constructed value.*

## 24

# READY FOR EVERY GOOD DEED

**Titus 3:1-7** Remind them to be... ready for every good deed, to malign no one, to be peaceable, gentle, showing every consideration for all people. For we also once were foolish ourselves, disobedient, deceived, enslaved to various lusts and pleasures, spending our life in malice and envy, hateful, hating one another. But when the kindness of God our Savior and His love for humanity appeared, He saved us, not on the basis of deeds which we have done in righteousness, but according to His mercy, by the washing of regeneration and renewing by the Holy Spirit, whom He poured out upon us richly through Jesus Christ our Savior, so that being justified by His grace we would be made heirs according to the hope of eternal life.

In a time of unprecedented social division and political acrimony, we will either conform to the dysfunctions of our culture, or we will be transformed by God to stand out as an attractive alternative. Jesus called His followers to be "salt and light" in the midst of a darkened and blinded world.

But what does it look like to be "salt and light" to our neighbors, colleagues, and family members who do not know Jesus? Paul offers a strong litmus test for us to consider:

**"Am I ready for every good deed?"** Tim Keller poses this challenge:

> Are we the kind of church of which [our community] says: *We don't share a lot of their beliefs, but I shudder to think of this [community] without them. They are such an important part of the community. They give so much! If they left we'd have to raise taxes because others won't give of themselves like they do* (emph. original).[13]

Tax-funded projects help many, but they always leave many needs in our communities unmet. What if Christians were known for voluntarily filling many of those gaps?

**"Do I malign others?"** The word "malign" comes from the Greek word from which we get our word "blaspheme." It refers to slandering or tearing down God or others made in His image. We expect people who are alienated from God to validate themselves by condemning others. Tragically, it is Christians who are so often known for their negative rants against those who disagree with their beliefs and ethics. How much better to follow the maxim of one wise author, who states, "If you have time to judge them, you have time to pray for them."

**"Am I peaceable?"** Paul writes, "If possible, so far as it depends upon you, be at peace with all people" (Romans 12:18). Unfortunately, many Christians use social media to express belligerence and incivility toward others—actions they probably would never express in person. Then again, research shows that such on-line incivility eventually makes us more rancorous in our face-to-face relationships. What might happen to Jesus' reputation if we prioritized genuine love and friendliness in both contexts?

**"Am I gentle, showing every consideration to all people?"** The term "gentle" is the opposite of being prickly and easily annoyed.

It describes winsome patience with others—their foibles, discourtesies, and even hostility. Likewise, we should be known for our genuine respect and consideration for "all people." What a contrast to the prejudice that permeates our society!

But how can we live this way? If you are like me, you realize this is humanly impossible. Left to my own motivation and resources, the best I can muster is superficial "niceness" toward others. But superficial niceness will not make others curious about Jesus. This sort of lifestyle requires supernatural motivation. This is why Paul continues in verses 4-7 to explain how God's grace is fully sufficient to transform us into people who represent Jesus well.[14] We can paraphrase these teachings in this way:

1. **"God initiated His kindness and mercy toward me when I least deserved it" (vv.3-5a).** God didn't rescue you because of any righteous deeds you performed toward Him or others. Far from it! Apart from God, we all lived lifestyles of selfish misery. No, God rescued you simply because He is merciful and kind. If God loved you in this way, certainly this kind of love can motivate you to respond in a similar way toward others who don't know Him.

2. **"God richly poured out His Spirit upon me" (vv.5b-6).** The Holy Spirit gave you new life and a new nature the moment you turned to Christ. His Spirit now indwells you, pouring God's love into your heart (Romans 5:5). Right at this moment, He can empower you to practically communicate His love to people who are far from Him. Your role? Simply present yourself to God as an instrument in His mighty hand. Ask His Spirit to guide and empower you (Romans 6:13). With such supernatural provision, showing others the kindness God has shown you becomes an exciting adventure!

3. **"God has guaranteed me eternal life in His kingdom" (v.7).** God has justified you as an undeserved gift. This is the basis upon which God adopts you as His child, who is now an heir of the everlasting kingdom that He will bring when Jesus returns. Since you can be confident you will spend all eternity enjoying

God's kingdom, certainly you can represent Him well during the short time you live in this fallen world! As Paul says elsewhere, "I consider that the sufferings of this present time are not worthy to be compared to the glory that is to be revealed to us" (Romans 8:18).

---

*Lord Jesus, I want to represent You well to those who are far from You—but this is beyond my ability. Thank You for rescuing me from a life of selfish misery. Thank You for showing me mercy when I deserved judgment, for sending Your Spirit to give me new life when I deserved death, and for giving me a secure future in Your eternal kingdom when I deserved separation from You. Open the eyes of my heart today to be empowered by Your grace, so that I may give to others the love You have lavished upon me.*

# 25

# MY WORD WILL NOT RETURN EMPTY

**Isaiah 6:9-10** "Go, and tell this people: 'Keep on listening, but do not perceive; keep on looking, but do not understand.' Render the hearts of this people insensitive, their ears dull, and their eyes dim. Otherwise they might see with their eyes, hear with their ears, understand with their hearts, and return and be healed."

**Isaiah 55:10-11** "For as the rain and the snow come down from heaven, and do not return there without watering the earth and making it bear and sprout, and furnishing seed to the sower and bread to the eater; so will My word be which goes forth from My mouth; it will not return to Me empty, without accomplishing what I desire, and without succeeding in the matter for which I sent it."

How can we reconcile these two apparently contradictory passages? In Isaiah 6, God indicates that none of Isaiah's contemporary hearers would heed his preaching. But in Isaiah 55, God promises that His Word through Isaiah would produce a rich harvest.

The key is to understand that the first passage refers to the *short-term* impact of Isaiah's preaching (i.e., in his lifetime), while the second passage refers to the *long-term* impact of Isaiah's preaching (i.e., in succeeding generations).

After seeing a vision of God's glory (Isaiah 6:1-7), God asked, "Who will go [speak] for us?" Isaiah immediately volunteered, saying, "Here am I. Send me!"

But then, God warned Isaiah not to expect a positive response from those who would hear his preaching. They had already hardened their hearts against God's word, and more preaching of His Word would not soften their hearts. Isaiah must have been taken aback by God's warning, so He asked, "How long should I expect to wait?" And God answered, "Until the people have been exiled and the land is desolate" (Isa. 6:11-12). Since this exile was not completed until after Isaiah died, his mission was to continue preaching God's word for the rest of his life—without expecting a single person to respond. By any reckoning, this would be a very tough assignment!

Later in Isaiah's ministry, though, God gave him a promise that richly compensated for a lifetime of apparently fruitless ministry: "[My word] will not return to Me empty, without accomplishing what I desire, and without succeeding in the matter for which I sent it" (Isaiah 55:11). Because Isaiah was proclaiming *God's* word, He could be sure it would eventually bear a rich harvest. This is because God's word is like a seed, carrying within itself the power to ultimately accomplish His redemptive purposes. As God said to Jeremiah, whose preaching ministry was also apparently fruitless, "I am watching over My Word to perform it" (Jeremiah 1:12). When we faithfully proclaim His Word, God ensures it will ultimately find its way to people who are willing to respond to it.

Surely Isaiah felt discouraged at times during his ministry: no one responded to a word he said. But how do you think Isaiah feels right now? How many people over the last 2,800 years have come to faith in Jesus by reading passages like Isaiah 53? How many believers have had their faith mightily strengthened by reading the book of Isaiah? Whatever guess we offer is likely to fall far, far short of reality. Today, decades of apparent fruitlessness are replaced by awe in what God has done through His word.

Over seven hundred years after Isaiah lived, the Messiah would experience a similar phenomenon. Although Jesus' teaching ministry appeared at first to be wildly popular, within three years the crowds had vanished. Indeed, the number of His followers dwindled to zero by the night of His arrest. It seemed His teaching had no lasting effect. Yet shortly after His resurrection and ascension, just days later, these same disciples turned back to Christ and saw thousands of people come to know Him. This same pattern has repeated itself countless times all over the world over the past two thousand years.

We are not divinely inspired prophets like Isaiah and Jeremiah, nor divinely inspired apostles like Paul and Peter. But we do have access to God's word. And this Word still possesses the same living power to produce a harvest—sooner or later. So, sow it generously! Share it as often as you have opportunity with those who don't know Christ (Colossians 4:5-6). Teach it to your children and grandchildren as you live your daily lives with them (Deuteronomy 6:7). Use it to encourage and counsel your brothers and sisters in Christ (Colossians 1:28; 3:16). God's word will *not* return empty! But will you sow it?

*Lord Jesus, thank You for the priceless privilege of being entrusted to share Your Word with others. Help me not to compare myself with others who may be more gifted in evangelism or preaching or teaching. Help me to be faithful to communicate Your Word the best I can to the people You have placed in my life. Thank You that Your Word is effectual—possessing within itself the power to germinate in human hearts. I thank You and praise You in advance for the eventual harvest You have promised. And I look forward to the day when I will be with You, when I will see fully and rejoice in Your harvest!*

# 26

# DON'T CALL EVERYTHING A CONSPIRACY

**Isaiah 8:11-15 NLT** The LORD has given me a strong warning not to think like everyone else does. He said, "Don't call everything a conspiracy, like they do, and don't live in dread of what frightens them. Make the LORD of Heaven's Armies holy in your life. He is the one you should fear. He is the one who should make you tremble. He will keep you safe. But to Israel and Judah he will be a stone that makes people stumble, a rock that makes them fall. And for the people of Jerusalem he will be a trap and a snare. Many will stumble and fall, never to rise again. They will be snared and captured."

At this moment in history, terror filled the hearts of the people of Judah. An invasion by the people of Israel and Aram loomed on the horizon. They threatened to kill the king of Judah and replace him with their own puppet ruler (Isaiah 7:6). Worse than this, the Assyrians—the greatest superpower of their time—stood right behind these nations. They were like a mighty hurricane, crashing across the known world and decimating every nation in sight (Isaiah 8:7). In the midst of this political instability, conspiracy theories began to circulate.

Conspiracy theories thrive during times of social upheaval. They give their adherents a false sense of security. It feels good to be "in the know," to understand the *real* story, and to know who the *real*, hidden enemies are. It makes people feel like they have a better chance of navigating the threats and fears ahead. Conspiracy theories appeal to us because they make people the enemy and help us to justify blaming them for our predicaments.

Not much has changed in the last couple thousand years. We live in a society in which conspiracy theories abound. Political polarization, racial unrest, a pandemic, mob violence—these and other factors have converged to create a sense of instability that may be unprecedented in our lifetimes. One of the worst outcomes is a rising cultural consensus that there is no such thing as objective truth, which only exacerbates the instability.

The internet gives us unparalleled access to information. But it has become more and more difficult to discern which is factual and helpful, and which is harmful speculation or even purposeful lies. Conspiracy theories are one form of this speculation to which we have easy access. Now more than ever, it is easy to go down one of these "rabbit holes" that promise us a false sense of security and moral superiority.

God acknowledges that there are real conspiracies (unlawful human alliances), and He condemns them. The Old Testament uses "conspiracy" in this way several times.[15] But in Isaiah 8, the issue is not whether or not a particular conspiracy exists (some do; some don't), or how harmful it may be (some may be very harmful; others may be innocuous). The issue is that God does not want His people to *focus* on conspiracies. God says, "Don't call everything a conspiracy, like they do, and don't live in dread of what frightens them" (Isaiah 8:12 NLT). An obsession over any conspiracy theory claims our hearts and minds and ultimately leads us down a dangerous and destructive path. God gives us several reasons why we should heed this solemn warning:

1. **"Make the LORD of Heaven's Armies holy in your life" (v.13).** God is the ultimate and unique object of our trust. He is the "Lord of *Heaven's Armies*," the One who rules over the whole universe, including a vast multitude of angels. Furthermore, He is the "*Lord of Heaven's Armies*," the God who entered into a solemn covenant with His people,[16] who promised to care for them, and who has proven Himself faithful to His promises. It is understandable that people who do not belong to God would turn to conspiracy theories during turbulent times. But how can God's very own people look to anyone or anything other than Him for their ultimate security? Surrendering our security in God for a conspiracy theory is to trade away our royal birthright for a mess of pottage!

2. **"He is the one you should fear. He is the one who should make you tremble. He will keep you safe" (vv.13b-14a).** The fear of God expels our other fears.[17] The "fear of God" does not refer to the cringing terror of a dangerous authority figure. Throughout the Old Testament, the fear of God is synonymous with awe-inspiring reverence. It leads to an increasing trust in God's proven love, forgiveness, and faithfulness. The more we focus on any other fear, the more threatening it becomes, and the more tempted we become to resort to conspiratorial thinking to protect ourselves.

Rip your focus off such things. Put your focus on God—where it belongs. Focus on the reality of God, His promises, and His proven record of faithfulness. As you do this, God "grows bigger" in your field of vision, even as human threats grow smaller. God "will keep you safe," guarding your heart and mind with a peace that surpasses human comprehension (Philippians 4:7).

3. **"But to Israel and Judah he will be a stone that makes people stumble, a rock that makes them fall. And for the people of Jerusalem he will be a trap and a snare. Many will stumble and fall, never to rise again. They will be snared and captured" (vv.14-15).** God warned the Israelites that if they persisted in focusing on conspiracy theories, He would discipline them by giving them over to the object of their fears. How sad it is to see

Christians needlessly dominated by maddening fears, when true peace, security, and faithfulness hover right at their fingertips.

---

*Lord Jesus, thank You that You have given me even greater promises than You gave the Israelites. Thank You that You promise me eternal life and a meaningful life of service in Your plan until the day that You return. Help me to focus on You instead of on my fears. Help me to trust in You, so that You may become my Sanctuary in my daily life.*

# 27

## DISCOURAGEMENT

**Isaiah 49:3-7 NLT** [God] said to me, "You are my servant, Israel, and you will bring me glory."
I replied, "But my work seems so useless! I have spent my strength for nothing and to no purpose. Yet I leave it all in the Lord's hand; I will trust God for my reward."
And now the Lord speaks—the one who formed me in my mother's womb to be his servant, who commissioned me to bring Israel back to him. The Lord has honored me, and my God has given me strength. He says, "You will do more than restore the people of Israel to me. I will make you a light to the Gentiles, and you will bring my salvation to the ends of the earth."
The Lord, the Redeemer and Holy One of Israel, says to the one who is despised and rejected by the nations, to the one who is the servant of rulers: "Kings will stand at attention when you pass by. Princes will also bow low because of the Lord, the faithful one, the Holy One of Israel, who has chosen you."

All who follow God become deeply discouraged at times. We face a special temptation in this area when our attempts to serve God seem to amount to nothing. Have you ever felt that your work for the Lord is pointless and futile? How can we recover from this kind of discouragement?

Isaiah 49 describes a despondent speaker. But who is he? In verse 3, he identifies with the nation of Israel. Yet verse 6 states that He will restore the nation of Israel. This mysterious figure—called the Suffering Servant—is none other than Jesus Christ. Since He arose from the nation of Israel, He represents the nation in a unique way. He is God's Servant who would come to bring salvation to the entire world through His death and resurrection (see Isaiah 42, 49, 50, 53).[18]

Does this mean that Jesus suffered from discouragement? At some point (evidently late in His public ministry), Jesus looked at His years of service and felt overwhelmed by this thought: "My work seems so useless! I have spent my strength for nothing and to no purpose" (verse 4 NLT). He had come to rescue His own people, yet they had despised and rejected Him (verse 7). How comforting it is to know that Jesus, the One who never sinned, was plagued with the same thoughts and feelings which sometimes overwhelm us! This must mean that it isn't intrinsically unspiritual to experience discouragement like this from time to time.

Like the spread of a fungus or mold, discouragement seems to grow best in the dark. But look at Jesus: He openly admitted these feelings to Himself and to God the Father. It does no good to simply put on a happy face. Far better to admit it and bring it out into the light. Pour it out to God. He can bear it for you, and He can help you out of it.

Jesus teaches another valuable lesson about dealing with discouragement: Balance honesty with fidelity. Jesus openly shared His feelings, but He never let them control His choices. Jesus felt that His work was "useless" and had amounted to "nothing." But then He says the crucial word *yet*. That one word speaks volumes. It reflects His refusal to allow His discouragement to drown out God's voice: "Yet I leave it all in the LORD's hand; I will trust God for my reward" (verse 4). And what was God's estimation of Jesus' ministry? "I will make you a light to the Gentiles, and you will bring my salvation to the ends of the earth" (verse 6). Jesus concluded that He did not see the whole picture, and He chose to trust the words of the One who did.

When you face an extended time of disillusionment or even despair, begin by telling God what you think and feel. But be sure to also say *yet*. Conclude your time in prayer by affirming to God that what He says about you is true. When you received Jesus, you also received many, many promises from God. He loves you like a beloved child (Romans 8:14-16). Not long from now, you will receive an eternal inheritance (Romans 8:17-18). Even your current discouragement will ultimately be worked for good (Romans 8:28). If your feelings say one thing, but divine facts say another, which is true? Choosing to trust God's words is not just an exercise in positive thinking; it is an affirmation of what is actually true.

When Jesus was in the Garden of Gethsemane, we see this same pattern. He admitted to His disciples, "My soul is deeply grieved, even to the point of death" (Matthew 26:38). He poured out His feelings of depression and fear to His Father, even saying, "If it is possible, let this cup pass from Me" (Matthew 26:39). But He ended His prayer with the word, "Yet…" He prayed, "Yet not as I will, but as You will." He chose to obey divine facts rather than personal fears. And as He prayed in this way, angels came and strengthened Him (Luke 22:43).

No matter how discouraged you may feel today, you can follow Jesus' example. You can express your discouragements to yourself and to God. Afterwards, God will often lead you to share with key friends who can give you counsel and encouragement to press on. But during these times, never forget to add the key word, "Yet…" You can tell God: "I'm feeling burdened with discouragement… Yet, I choose to trust Your Word more than how I feel." As you relate to God in this way, His Spirit will lessen the weight of your discouragement. And in His own perfect timing, God will encourage your heart to go on serving Him!

*Lord Jesus, I am amazed and comforted by the knowledge that You have shared in my experience of discouragement. Surely I can draw near to You—not as an unsympathetic authority figure, but as One who has been tempted in all ways as I have been tempted. Thank You for leading the way in choosing to trust Your Father's words over Your feelings of discouragement. Uplift and strengthen me today as I choose to respond to Your promises.*

# 28

# PRIDE AND HUMILITY

**Isaiah 65:5 NLT** "They say to each other, 'Don't come too close or you will defile me! I am holier than you!' These people are a stench in my nostrils, an acrid smell that never goes away."

**Isaiah 66:2 NLT** "My hands have made both heaven and earth; they and everything in them are mine. I, the Lord, have spoken! I will bless those who have humble and contrite hearts, who tremble at my word."

God manifests very different responses to our attitude toward him and others. A "holier than thou" attitude repulses God, but an attitude of humble instruction brings blessing from Him.

It is not as though God rejects us if we have ever had a self-righteous attitude. Nor is it that God owes us His blessing if we have ever heeded His Word. We are all sinners who deserve God's judgment, and we are accepted by Him only through our faith in the gracious gift of His Son. Think rather of these two attitudes as our hearts' most basic responses to God: pride and humility.

Pride manifests itself most commonly not in blasphemous raging against God, but in self-righteous judgment against others. Our sinful hearts exalt themselves more often by criticizing others' faults than by overt boasting. When I look back on my inner thought-life for the day, it is sobering to realize how many of my thoughts were essentially what Isaiah wrote: "Don't come too close or you will defile me! I am holier than you!" (Isaiah 65:5 NLT). Almost anything can serve as fodder for my self-righteous judgment: political opinions, personality eccentricities, mispronounced words, physical imperfections, minor interruptions—this smoldering self-righteousness creates smoke in God's nostrils.

Self-righteous pride doesn't just keep others away, but it keeps us from drawing near to God Himself. After all, what does pride communicate? Whether we realize it or not, pride stiff-arms God by saying, "I don't need Your mercy because I am better than other people." Any honest person realizes how much this attitude infects him. But this basic self-awareness ignores the most insidious thing about pride: the more it dominates our hearts, the less we realize its presence and harmful effects.

Maybe this is why Jesus was so strong in His exposure and denunciation of self-righteous pride. He reserved His severest rebukes for the scribes and Pharisees (Matthew 23). He told parables that rebuked self-righteous attitudes toward common sinners (Luke 15). He exposed the Pharisees' "Thank You that I am not like other people" prayers as boasts that prevented God from accepting them (Luke 18:9-14). Some people think Jesus spoke this way because He was disgusted with them. But I believe He spoke in love. He was trying to wake them up from their self-righteous slumber. He has certainly needed to speak this way to me to wake me up from the blindness of my pride!

On the other hand, God *always* looks with favor on a humble heart. As James says, "God is opposed to the proud, but He gives grace to the humble" (James 4:6). Read that again: When God finds a humble heart, He *always* exalts it. As Peter says, "Humble yourselves under the mighty hand of God, that He may exalt you at the proper time" (1 Peter 5:6). To the tax-collector who prayed,

"God be merciful to me, the sinner," Jesus promised that He went home justified—granted right standing with God (Luke 18:13).

Our greatest need in life is a humble heart. Do you believe that? Most of us don't. We think that our biggest need is for people or circumstances to change. Not true. If we have a humble heart, we have God's favor, and that is all anyone could ever need.

But we cannot self-generate humility any more than we can self-eradicate pride. However, we can agree with God and ask Him to break our pride and to work humility into our hearts. We can also cooperate with Him as He describes what humility looks like. For instance, Isaiah writes that he who is humble is "contrite in spirit and trembles at My word" (Isaiah 66:2).

A contrite spirit is a heart that receives God's correction without excuses, rationalizations, or blame-shifting. The self-righteous criticisms of the self-righteous most often camouflage God's correction. A contrite heart, however, receives God's correction and casts itself on God's mercy alone. Such people will never be disappointed. The joy of God's mercy swallows up the pain of being wrong. A contrite heart is secure because it is loved by God for Christ's righteousness, rather than the unstable foundation of self-righteousness.

According to God, the person with a humble heart "trembles at My word." This is not the trembling of a servile fear of punishment. It is the trembling of a heart that thrills to listen to the One who is so gracious. To tremble at God's word is to fear Him in the biblical sense: "If You, LORD, should mark iniquities, O Lord, who could stand? But there is forgiveness with You, that You may be feared" (Psalm 130:3-4). A humble soul rejoices in God's forgiveness and regards His instruction as a precious gift of His love.

If you are a child of God, there will be a war in your soul today between these two attitudes. You cannot prevent this internal conflict, but you can say to God: "I want the humility that you offer to win." You can ask for God's help to choose humility in the concrete situations that emerge. Don't miss this opportunity when it arises. God will give you grace and exalt you!

---

*Thank You, Lord Jesus, that You expose my pride through Your perfect humility. Thank You that You humbled Yourself to death on a cross to pay the just penalty of my pride. Help me today to turn away from a "holier-than-thou" attitude, and teach me how to have a humble heart that trembles at Your word.*

# 29

## SERVING GOD IN OLD AGE

**Psalm 71:14-18** As for me, I will hope continually, and will praise You yet more and more. My mouth shall tell of Your righteousness and of Your salvation all day long; for I do not know the sum of them. I will come with the mighty deeds of the LORD God; I will make mention of Your righteousness, Yours alone. O God, You have taught me from my youth, and I still declare Your wondrous deeds. And even when I am old and gray, O God, do not forsake me, until I declare Your strength to this generation, Your power to all who are to come.

**Psalm 92:12-15** The righteous man will flourish like the palm tree, he will grow like a cedar in Lebanon. Planted in the house of the Lord, they will flourish in the courts of our God. They will still yield fruit in old age; they shall be full of sap and very green, to declare that the LORD is upright; He is my rock, and there is no unrighteousness in Him.

---

I remember as a young, teenage Christian how much I looked up to the Christians who had been walking with God for many years. What they communicated through their examples and words inspired me with hope that I could become more godly if

I just hung in there. Their obvious love for God inspired me that my relationship with Him need never grow stale or cold. Their confidence in God's faithfulness through many adversities and failures assured me that I could count on the same God as I walked into an unknown future.

We have an opportunity to glorify God throughout life—including in our old age. God promises that He has prepared good works for us to walk in throughout our entire lives (Ephesians 2:10). This promise isn't limited to our youth or middle age—but to our *entire* lives.

The psalmist concurs. He doesn't speak negatively about the "old and gray." God promises vitality and fruitfulness for every person who follows Him to the end of their lives. What a welcome word to those of us who live in a culture that prizes youth and disparages old age! It is also a challenging word to those of us who may be tempted to believe the lie that this stage of life is good for nothing besides selfish leisure. God provides many promises, encouragement, and vision to those walking this stage of their lives.

**Those in old age are called "righteous" (Psalm 92:12).** The "righteous man" does not refer only to super-saints; it refers to all whom God has declared to be in right standing with Him—justified through faith in Jesus Christ (Galatians 2:16).

**Those in old age are called a "cedar of Lebanon" (Psalm 92:12).** Palm trees flourish because they grow near to water. Much like our redwoods, the cedars of Lebanon grew tall because they received abundant moisture from the Mediterranean Sea. What a beautiful picture of the spiritual vitality and stature that can characterize our lives because we are connected to Jesus Christ, the Source of living water! (John 7:37-39)

**Those in old age are "planted in the house of the Lord… (so they can) flourish in the courts of our God" (Psalm 92:13).** In the old covenant, people met God in the Temple—or the "house of the Lord." Now, Jesus is our new Temple. Whatever diminished capacities or infirmities we may experience, we have the most important asset: We have personal access to God through Jesus. We are indwelt by God's Spirit, who alone imparts spiritual hope and peace and joy regardless of our age or physical health (Romans 15:13).

**Those in old age "still yield fruit" and "shall be full of sap and very green" (Psalm 92:14).** This is yet another picture of vitality and productivity—specifically promised to those of us who are "in old age!" Like Paul, we can say, "Though our outer man is decaying, yet our inner man is being renewed day by day" (2 Corinthians 4:16). We can count on a daily fresh supply of God's empowerment to serve Him.

**Those in old age can praise God more and more as they keep learning about His salvation (Psalm 71:14-15).** For as long as we live in this world, we can continue to grow in our understanding and appreciation of what God has given us through Jesus. Here indeed are "the unfathomable riches in Christ" (Ephesians 3:8)! Even in eternity, we will never fully plumb the depths of God's kindness (see Ephesians 2:7). But we can keep increasing in our praise to God in this life. This pleases Him, fulfills us, and attracts others to Him!

**Those in old age can declare the goodness and faithfulness of God, especially to those who are much younger than them (Psalm 92:15; 71:17-18).** Older Christians often mistakenly think they have nothing spiritually important to offer younger people, or that younger people will not want to receive anything we do offer. But the longer you have walked with God, the more you have experienced His wisdom and His goodness. What could be more important and helpful for anyone who loves God—regardless of their age?

One of the most valuable treasures we have to offer others is our personal testimony that "God is my Rock, and there is no unrighteousness in Him" (92:15). And we can all offer this precious gift to others right up to the moment when we go to be with God!

*Thank You, Lord Jesus, for the exciting vision You give us for this final stage of our lives! Thank You that we are righteous in Your sight through our simple faith in Your death for our sins. Thank You that You promise to keep renewing us spiritually even as we weaken physically. Thank You for giving us a testimony about Your goodness that will be helpful to many other people. Help us this day, Lord, to praise You for these promises, and to serve You with a glad heart wherever You have placed us.*

# 30

# HOW GREAT ARE YOUR WORKS

**Psalm 92:1-5** It is good to give thanks to the Lord and to sing praises to Your name, O Most High; to declare Your lovingkindness in the morning and Your faithfulness by night, with the ten-stringed lute and with the harp, with resounding music upon the lyre. For You, O Lord, have made me glad by what You have done, I will sing for joy at the works of Your hands. How great are Your works, O Lord! Your thoughts are very deep.

The title of this Psalm tells us that it was composed as a "song for the Sabbath day." How good it is to set aside regular time to rest in God's care, and what better way to do this than to reflect on God's character? As Derek Kidner comments:

> It is *right* to give God thanks and sing His praise; but here we go further and call it *good*: good… in the sense that it uplifts and liberates us. We are made glad by the works of God and by His ways in proportion as we give our minds and voices to expressing the wonder of them."[19]

This act of praise rips our eyes off ourselves and others and focuses them on God, who will refresh and reinvigorate our souls.

The psalmist invites us to focus on two wondrous aspects of God: His gracious character and His work as Creator.

**1. The psalmist encourages us to praise God for His gracious character.** The psalmist refers to God's "lovingkindness" (*hesed*) and "faithfulness" (*emunah*). These words are the Old Testament's favorite terms for what the New Testament calls God's "grace." The "lovingkindness" (*hesed*) refers to a "loving loyalty" to His people, despite our many sins and failings (Exodus 34:6-7). This "lovingkindness" (*hesed*) fills God's nature. God is utterly faithful to us, despite the vacillations in our faithfulness to Him (2 Timothy 2:13).

Because God's gracious and faithful character is so different from ours, we are prone to almost unconsciously project onto Him our own ungracious and unfaithful image. When we do this, the thought of God arouses anxiety—which makes us want to avoid His presence. Maybe this is why the psalmist needed to learn to declare to *himself* God's graciousness and faithfulness at the beginning and the end of each day.

Recall what God says about Himself in His word. Remember how God has proven His love to you in your own life. And then, thank Him and praise Him in your own words. What a difference it makes to bookend each day with this reminder! Then we can go forward into the day—or we can go to sleep—with a peace rooted in God's unchanging love.

**2. The psalmist encourages us to praise God for His creation.** He extols God for the work of His creation: "what You have done" (v.4a), "the works of Your hands" (v.4b), and "Your works" (v.5). The author keenly observes the natural world, following the trail of its many glories back to its Source—the Creator. The natural world overflows with breathtaking beauty. But if the creation is this beautiful, how much more beautiful must its Creator be? (Psalm 27:4)

When we look at the Great Pyramids of Giza, we stand in awe

of the power and might of the pharaohs who built such massive masterpieces. But the pyramids are no more than little pebbles compared to the vastness of the physical universe. When we ponder the incredible immensity of nature, it leads us to ask how immense God must be to create such immensity! The psalmist is particularly impressed with the intricate design of nature: "How great are Your works, O Lord; Your thoughts are very deep" (v.5). Elsewhere, the psalmist says, "O Lord, how many are Your works! In wisdom You have made them all; the earth is full of Your possessions" (Psalm 104:24). How profound must be the intelligence of God to create the vast and intricate fabric of our universe!

Many modern American Christians forfeit the soul nourishment that comes from praising God for His creation. Most of us live in cities, where human construction is exaggerated, and God's handiwork is diminished. God's handiwork is still there in the city, but we must take the time and cultivate intentional attentiveness to appreciate it and follow its trail back to God.

Go for a walk and take time to reflect upon what you see in God's creation. Ask God to help you to appreciate what He has created. Observe the trees and the birds. Admire the sky. Inhale the scent of living things. Give thanks and praise to God for these precious gifts! Remind yourself that the God who created such natural beauty is also the same God who created you, loves you, and promises to care for you. The same God who created the natural world has kept His promises to send His Son, Jesus Christ, to give Himself for the penalty of your sins. And this same God will send His Son to remake this world and everything in it so that we can fully know and enjoy Him. Today is one step closer to this glorious future for all who have entrusted themselves to Jesus.

It is indeed good to give thanks to the Lord and to sing praises to His name!

*Thank You, Lord, that Your lovingkindness remains constant, despite my many outbursts of selfishness. Your faithfulness is my great foundation on which I can depend, despite my frequent emotional fluctuations. Your creation is a daily reminder of Your infinite beauty and might and intelligence. You gave my soul a capacity to thank You and praise You. And now, through Your Son Jesus, I know Whom to thank and praise! Help me this day to demonstrate Your graciousness and faithfulness to the people who will cross my path.*

# 31

## IS THIS NOT A BURNING STICK?

**Zechariah 3:1-5** Then he showed me Joshua the high priest standing before the angel of the LORD, and Satan standing at his right hand to accuse him. The LORD said to Satan, "The LORD rebuke you, Satan! Indeed, the LORD who has chosen Jerusalem rebuke you! Is this not a burning stick plucked from the fire?" Now Joshua was clothed with filthy garments and standing before the angel. He spoke and said to those who were standing before him, saying, "Remove the filthy garments from him." Again he said to Joshua, "See, I have taken your iniquity away from you and will clothe you with festal robes." Then I said, "Let them put a clean turban on his head." So they put a clean turban on his head and clothed him with garments, while the angel of the LORD was standing by.

---

Have you ever plucked a burning stick from a campfire? The flaming stick consumes itself from within, but it also disintegrates from the flames that surround it. This metaphor describes Joshua's predicament. As the high priest, he lit his life on fire from *within* by his own sinful choices. But the nation of Israel also lit his life on fire from *without* because of their multi-generational rebellion against God. Isaiah understood both the personal and social effects of sin. He cried out to God, "Woe is me, for I am ruined! Because I am a man of unclean lips, *and* I live among a people of unclean lips" (Isaiah 6:5).

Left to himself, Joshua faced the doom of incineration. Yet God plucked him from the fire, forgave him of the guilt of his many sins, and commissioned him to be His representative. The angel of the Lord mysteriously intervened in Joshua's rescue. *He* was the one to rebuke Satan's accusations. *He* removed Joshua's guilt. *He* clothed Joshua in clean festal robes and put a priest's turban on his head. Today we know the identity of this divine messenger: He is the Lord Jesus Christ. His death on the cross was the basis of Joshua's rescue and reclamation.

Can you relate to God's description of Joshua being a "burning stick plucked from the fire"? Recently, God reminded me that this is an apt description of my own life.

Before God rescued me through Jesus, my life was burning down. I had chosen to live independently from God—truly, to be my own god. At first, this path seemed wise and liberating. But each choice in this direction only ignited another flame that charred my soul. The apostle Paul describes it this way, "For we also once were foolish ourselves, disobedient, deceived, enslaved to various lusts and pleasures, spending our life in malice and envy, hateful, hating one another" (Titus 3:3). My life was on track to burn to the ground.

But it wasn't just my own sinful choices that set my life aflame. I was also born into a family on fire. Generations of godlessness resulted in a whirlpool of fiery dysfunction. God created the family to be a powerful "system" that communicates His life and love to its members. But when a family departs from God, it becomes a death-dealing system that ripples down through the generations. Except for two believers in my own extended family, our system was very broken. And apart from God's rescue, the dysfunctional fire would continue unabated.

Who can explain the mercy of God, that He would rescue someone like me—a burning stick in the midst of a great fire? I said "Yes" to Him when He came to rescue me. But only the great mercy of God made this rescue possible. When one is perishing inside a burning house, he does not boast that he allowed a firefighter to carry him to safety. Rather, he marvels that someone would risk his own life to save one so utterly doomed! In the same way, Paul says: "But when the kindness of God our Savior and His love for us appeared, He saved us, not on the basis of deeds which we have done in righteousness, but according to His mercy... (which) He poured out upon us richly through Jesus Christ our Savior" (Titus 3:4-6).

God plucked a burning stick like me from the fire. But He did not stop there. He made me His child, and He gave me a unique role in representing Him in this broken world. Why would He entrust such a privilege to someone like me? When I was a young believer, I thought God was lucky to have me. But the more I go on with God, the more amazed I am that He works through me. As one author wrote:

> [God] does use me. But... the axe cannot boast of the trees it has cut down. It could do nothing but for the woodsman. He made it, he sharpened it, and he used it. The moment he throws it aside, it becomes only iron. O that I may never lose sight of this.[20]

---

*Thank You, Lord Jesus, for your great mercy. Like Joshua, I am a burning stick plucked from the fire. Help me to live today as a grateful recipient of Your mercy. Work through me today to offer Your mercy to others.*

# ENDNOTES

1. This pattern of *See-Feel-Act* is also a key element in Jesus' two most famous parables—the Good Samaritan (see Luke 10:33,34) and the Prodigal Son (see Luke 15:20).

2. Darrell L. Bock, *The NIV Application Commentary: Luke* (Zondervan, 1996), p. 310.

3. Jack Miller, *Outgrowing the Ingrown Church* (Zondervan, 1986), p. 96.

4. O. Hallesby, *Prayer* (Augsburg, 1975), p. 21.

5. Andrew Murray, *With Christ in the School of Prayer* (London: James Nisbet & Co., 1887), pp. 52-53.

6. C. S. Lewis, *Letters to Malcom, Chiefly on Prayer* (Harcourt Brace & Company, 1992), p. 124.

7. Some commentators view these participles as describing *results* of being filled with the Spirit (in contrast to "dissipation"), rather than *means* of being filled with the Spirit. But there are several reasons why Paul used them as participles of *means*. The parallel

passage in Colossians 3:16 ("teaching," "admonishing," "giving thanks") clearly explains *how* to "let the word of Christ richly dwell within you."

8. Elisabeth Kübler-Ross, *Death: The Final Stage of Growth* (Scribner, 1997).

9. Ajith Fernando, *Spiritual Living in a Secular World* (Zondervan, 1993), p. 153.

10. Wayne A. Grudem, *1 Peter: An Introduction and Commentary* (Tyndale, 2009), p. 181.

11. C. S. Lewis, *The Weight of Glory* (HarperCollins, 2001), p. 170.

12. William R. Newell, "A Few Words about Grace," in *Romans, Verse by Verse* (Kregel Classics, 1994), pp. 245-9.

13. Tim Keller, "The Gospel and the Supremacy of Christ in a Postmodern World," in John Piper and Justin Taylor (general editors), *The Supremacy of Christ in a Postmodern World* (Crossway Books, 2007), p.122.

14. "For" in verse 3 explains the connection between verses 1-2 and verses 3-7: It is the grace that God has shown us that motivates and empowers us to love non-Christians.

15. See 2 Samuel 15:12; 1 Kings 16:20; 2 Kings 12:20; 14:19; 15:15, 30; 17:4; Jeremiah 11:9; Ezekiel 22:25.

16. The Hebrew word for "Lord" is *Yahweh*, which is the name God used for Himself when He promised Moses that He would deliver the Israelites from Egypt because He had chosen them to be His people (see Exodus 3). This use of the name for God emphasizes that He is a covenant-making and promise-keeping God.

17. The psalmist also writes, "I sought the Lord, and He answered me, and delivered me from all my fears… The angel of the Lord encamps around those who fear Him, and rescues them" (Psalm 34:4, 7).

**18.** After Isaiah 49:6, the Servant is always distinguished from the nation of Israel (see Isaiah 53). Moreover, the Servant brings "salvation to the ends of the earth." Israel never accomplished this, but Jesus is in the process of accomplishing this (Matthew 24:14).

**19.** Derek Kidner, *Psalms 73-150: An Introduction and Commentary*, Vol. 16 (InterVarsity Press, 1975), pp. 366-367.

**20.** Samuel Brengle, cited in Oswald Sanders, *Spiritual Leadership* (Moody Press, 1994), p. 62.

# OTHER TITLES BY GARY DELASHMUTT

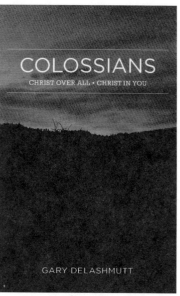